Praise for *Engaged*

"Mix timeless wisdom with modern neuroscience and you get *Engaged,* a terrific new book from Amy Brann. Upon immersing yourself in this evidence-based approach, you'll see and understand organizational behavior in an entirely new light and you'll be well equipped to elevate your people, your team and your bottom line. Both insightful and practical, this is a very relevant book!"

— **Stephen M. R. Covey**, author of *The New York Times* and # 1 *Wall Street Journal* bestselling book, *The Speed of Trust*, and co-author of *Smart Trust*

"*Engaged* takes contemporary neuroscience theory and applies insights that will equip organizations to be both productive and fulfilling places to work. Engaged brains can make all the difference."

— **Professor John Parkinson**, *Head of School of Psychology, Bangor University*

"*Engaged* tackles with ease some of the most uncomfortably complex topics facing many modern organizations and business leaders. Drawing on a wealth of experience from people in the know, this book weaves a story using neuroscience as the thread, systematically demystifying difficult concepts. What I love about it is that you can take exactly what you need from it – whether it is something for the here and now from the 'What Can I do Today' feature, or a more detailed insight for example into the role of neurotransmitters in healthy brain function. *Engaged* is an invaluable companion for business champions of change."

— **Paul Carter**, *Behavioral Neuropsychologist*

"Amy & Synaptic Potential have some really interesting ideas and approaches to organizational culture and engagement – I look forward to watching them develop even further with practical implementation."

— **Cathy Brown**, *Exec Director, Engage for Success*

"*Engaged* is as inspiring as it is insightful. It's a fact that an organization's culture and strategy dictate business success and it is always the people within organizations that determine the level of that success. *Engaged* is one of those great books that brings all of that together in such a meaningful way. The book is underpinned with science and practical examples, which can be applied in your organization right now. It's time to change the game and bring more meaning back to the workplace. You can start that process today by applying the insights from this fantastic book!"

— **Ben Whitter**, *Organisation and People Development Manager, The University of Nottingham Ningbo China*

"In *Engaged*, Amy Brann writes in her natural, accessible style, allowing Learning & Development professionals to understand and access concepts of neuroscience clearly and with relevance. In our time strapped world, it is so important to have full engagement in the workplace. In a profession which is often perceived to take people's engagement away from 'the work,' L&D can benefit with knowing more about creating engaging, less disruptive learning interventions. *Engaged* talks through how to do that, plus covers the all-important why too, and adds real stories from professionals in the L&D field.

Amy demonstrates, in *Engaged,* her experience and value to the study and research of neuroscience in a way which relates clearly to a business focus, particularly company cultures and environs. As L&D heads more towards consultative partnering within business rather than transactional course booking, having a better understanding of how to engage with business units and operational managers is of immense benefit. Just as L&D is going through a mind-set shift itself, the ideas in this book are pushing the whole of business to evolve better environments and philosophies; that cannot come soon enough, in my opinion."

— **Michelle Parry-Slater**, *L&D Director,*
Kairos Modern Learning

"ENGAGEMENT starts with capital 'E'— it is EVERYONE'S responsibility to keep self and others engaged and motivated. Using this book raises the awareness that it is not a manager's or an organization's duty – it is each single person in an organization to drive engagement in order to achieve better results. No excuses anymore: this book gives the reader evidence and practical tools to make engagement finally happen."

— **Dr. Tobias Kiefer**, *Global Learning Leader,*
EY & Chairman, Q595 GmbH

"With businesses under pressure to preform, they often overlook one of the most critical elements for their success: the correct utilization of human resources. Achieving optimization and performance requires understanding the underpinning of human cognition and using it to shape businesses. This book understands that most businesses today actually work against the nature of human performance, and that taking insights from neuroscience can really improve their performance. Read this book to gain understanding of these issues and how to move forward."

— **Dr. Itiel Dror**, *University College London and*
Cognitive Consultants International

The Neuroscience of **Business**

The Neuroscience of Business series

Neuroscience is changing our understanding of how the human brain works and how and why people behave the way they do. Properly understood, many of these insights could lead to profound changes in the way businesses interact with their employees and customers. The problem is that, until now, most of this research has been published in specialist journals and has not made its way to managers' desks. At the same time, however, business leaders and managers are faced with a plethora of extravagant claims based on misunderstood, or exaggerated, neuroscientific research.

Palgrave's The Neuroscience of Business series seeks to bridge the gap between rigorous science and the practical needs of business. For the first time this series will describe the practical managerial applications of this science in an accessible, but in-depth, way that is firmly underpinned by a clear explanation of the science behind the management actions proposed.

Series editors: Peter Chadwick and Roderick Millar
Series ISBN 978–11374–7832–0

Available now:
NEUROSCIENCE FOR LEADERSHIP
Tara Swart, Kitty Chisholm and Paul Brown

The Neuroscience behind Creating Productive People in Successful Organizations

Engaged

Amy Brann

Director, Synaptic Potential Ltd, UK

palgrave
macmillan

First published 2015 by
PALGRAVE MACMILLAN

Palgrave Macmillan in the UK is an imprint of Macmillan Publishers Limited, registered in England, company number 785998, of Houndmills, Basingstoke, Hampshire RG21 6XS.

Palgrave Macmillan in the US is a division of St Martin's Press LLC, 175 Fifth Avenue, New York, NY 10010.

Palgrave Macmillan is the global academic imprint of the above companies and has companies and representatives throughout the world.

Palgrave® and Macmillan® are registered trademarks in the United States, the United Kingdom, Europe and other countries.

ISBN 978–1–137–50040–3

This book is printed on paper suitable for recycling and made from fully managed and sustained forest sources. Logging, pulping and manufacturing processes are expected to conform to the environmental regulations of the country of origin.

A catalogue record for this book is available from the British Library.

A catalog record for this book is available from the Library of Congress.

Typeset by MPS Limited, Chennai, India.

Contents

Part IV How Do We Manage People?

List of Figures

About the Author

Amy Brann studied medicine at UCL before moving into the developing field of neuroscience and becoming a pioneer in the application of this cutting edge science to the art of developing people. She is an experienced executive coach (with over 12,000 hours of coaching behind her), a regular speaker on the application of neuroscience to leadership & HR, and is the director of Synaptic Potential, a consultancy offering neuroscience-based people management and leadership development services. She is the author of *Make Your Brain Work* and *Neuroscience for Coaches*.

Thanks

This book would not have been possible without the hard work, time, and willingness to share of so many people. I am very grateful to the scientists in labs around the world doing cutting-edge research and sharing this with us. I am also inspired and thankful to the people and organizations that are doing things with their people at the center of their focus.

Thank you to all the people who gave me their time freely and shared insights into their work: Andrea, Angela, Amy, Ben, David, Dean, Graham, Jabbar, Jane, Jo, Louisa, Martin, Misti, Neil, Raffaela, and others informally.

Special thanks go to Silviu Pop who patiently transcribed the many hours of interviews I conducted. His patience and professionalism were great to work with.

The team at Palgrave, Josie Taylor and Stephen Partridge, were always at the end of a phone and showed real commitment to the project.

Penultimate thanks to the friends who supported me during this intensive writing period and the team members at Synaptic Potential who kept things running.

Finally, thank you to my husband Stu who, despite his better judgment, supported me on writing a third book in three years. Thanks to my mum who helped us out a lot during this period. And thanks to little Jessica who, at two years of age, has taught me powerful lessons and brings us daily buckets of joy.

Further Resources

Please visit this book's website for further resources:

www.engagedbrains.com

Introduction

For the field of human resources a huge opportunity lies ahead: To reconnect with what being human means and to shape organizations to best work with this human nature.

Organizations should be more like preparing for parties.

There is normally a lot to do to set a party up to be fun, run smoothly and for people to enjoy themselves, in short, for it to be a success. People like their parties to be remembered for a long time. People love parties; they look forward to going, to meeting old friends, and making new ones. We could even say we are wired to party.

Don't get me wrong – all parties are different. There are the crazy ones where the music is loud and people dance a lot. There are the sophisticated dinner parties where everything is a little more cerebral. There are even the children's parties where the games are quite different and there are normally at least some tears. Preparing for each party is a little different; however, they do all tend to share some common traits.

The preparing-for-a-party bit can be quite a surreal experience. One of my favorite party preparation encounters lasted a long time. The intensive bit was for the five days before the party. Around 50 people came together to enjoy each other's company and carry out the final preparations. Some people knew each other from before, but many did not. Everyone came together with the big picture in mind: On Saturday there would be a big party with lots of guests. Everyone who came had different skills. Team players included a qualified electrician, great cooks, physically strong people, a couple with *lots* of energy, someone who was always happy to vacuum, another great at taking care of dogs, a couple of lovely beauticians, people who could drive, people who could make things look good, and many more.

There were some plans, certain things needed to happen, once people knew the overarching vision, though, they were quite self-sufficient. People seem to choose jobs that they were good at and enjoyed. Then they got on with it. There was no need for performance reviews. If people had a problem, they asked someone else for help.

Now, preparing for parties can be hard work for sure. Blowing up 30 balloons can take it out of you. Carrying heavy pieces of furniture, decorating four-tiered cakes, or working out solutions to problems that have just arisen can be taxing. However, some central themes, underpinned by neuroscience, seem to pull people through.

It feels great to step back during a party and know that you helped make this happen. Knowing that your contribution made a difference; being able to see the fruits of your hard work; hearing your friend thank you for showing up and being you – it all makes you feel good.

When you're preparing for a party, the very experience changes the chemicals that flood your brain and body. It is likely oxytocin, serotonin, and dopamine along with many more flow through you. The neural pathways you activate make it easier for them to be activated again. You strengthen your ability to do the things you do and be the way you are being for next time.

You connect with people. You feel more engaged because of this connection. The culture, or vibe perhaps in party-speak, shapes how things unfold. Certain ambiences and environments make the desirable vibe more likely. The way people connect is then affected and how they feel and are able to contribute is impacted.

People turn up *engaged*. They are self-motivated and the management creates itself. The "objectives" are met while at the same time people enjoy themselves. In this instance, they were excited on Monday and felt fulfilled on Friday. (The party also went wonderfully on Saturday.)

The Approach

Although it is likely we have just met, I have a favor to ask of you. That is to set aside your previous models of human resources and learning and development (henceforth HR and L&D). They were created before we understood what we do now about the brain. They could be holding you back. The paradigms, the rules, the systems, the processes – set them side – if you have a blank slate then after reading this book you might design things differently. In order to get the most out of your brain as you enjoy dancing with new ideas, you'll benefit from setting aside "what is" so you can fully play with "what could be."

Before I started writing books, whenever I bought one I would skip the introduction and jump right into the "juicy content." Now I'm tuned into the priming potential of an introduction.

I am driven by a deep desire to see people be happy. There is a lot to do in this lifetime, and feeling miserable every Sunday through to Wednesday because of work seems like a waste to me. I want to see people with a positive anticipation about Monday morning and feeling fulfilled on Friday afternoons. Positive psychology tells us that many good things come when people are in positive states. It doesn't make sense then for us to accept the current reality where so many people are unhappy about their work experience.

This book isn't designed or written to make anyone sound clever, it is to stimulate ideas and give you scientific backing to take those ideas to people who, together with, you can transform what exists already into something even better. Most HR and L&D professionals, leaders, and managers don't have the capacity to go through hundreds of scientific papers to evaluate their current ways of shaping their organization. This resource has started the hard work for you, good luck in the next stage of your journey.

Why Is Neuroscience so Exciting?

Neuroscience is providing insights into how we work. Organizations have their own agendas and goals. They also have their own ways of trying to advance towards those goals. Neuroscience challenges some of the basic ethoses that are still being taught in business schools.

Neuroscience, the scientific study of the brain, has experts around the world uncovering new information about how the brain works. To scale up the applications from neuroscience often takes some reflection and translation. The challenges some people make to the practice of applying neuroscience, in particular, suggesting neuroscience is concerned with the micro, carry weight, but the firmer understanding of the micro enables us to better understand and place the macro behaviors.

At Synaptic Potential, our belief is that neuroscience adds another layer of valuable information. We use it in combination with insights from other disciplines, such as psychology, behavioral science, positive psychology, neuroeconomics, and more. This approach enables us to see more clearly than relying on only one lens. In the past, disciplines were much more segregated, like in organizations where departments work in silos. Thankfully we're seeing much more interdisciplinary collaboration. This is accelerating our understanding of people and ability to work more effectively with them.

Why Is Neuroscience Fundamental to HR and L&D?

As often happens, asking why neuroscience is fundamental to HR and L&D, which happens frequently, misdirects our attention. The reality is that neuroscience is fundamental to the *whole* organization. Many believe one of the challenges HR has faced is that it has been relegated to an administrative function rather than a strategic one.[1] The ideal is for HR to work synergistically with and for the organization. This makes logical sense and has been correlated with better business results. What form that needs to take practically is not prescribed by neuroscience. The aim of the business partner model developed by Ulrich is "to help HR professionals integrate more thoroughly into business processes and to align their day-to-day work with business outcomes."[2] That sounds like a good aim. It is possible there may be more creative ways of achieving that goal. I know this may sound crazy but some organizations do not even have a "HR function."

Back to the (Imperfect) Question...

Imagine you are driving along a long road. You have a destination you planned to reach and wanted a smooth journey with minimal discomfort. Your car breaks down. Luckily, two people stop to help you out. The first person had watched a program on pistons last night. He starts saying some things that indicate he knows what he is talking about – but only in relation to pistons. The second person, on the other hand, is a mechanic. She spends her days with the whole engine, she knows all the components well and how they interact. Who would you rather help fix your car? Now, it may just be that you've run out of oil and your warning light has broken. It may however be more complex.

With humans it is often more complex. An individual is just that. One problem in organizations is that we are often trying to systemize things and end up treating people as if they are someone they are not. Motivation, how we make decisions, what is rewarding to us, how to get the best out of us, how we learn – these are all topics that can show variation between individuals. In this book, we will look at some themes. We will turn to the scientific disciplines that can inform us about how fundamentally people are motivated, how they make decisions, and how to get the best out of them. Suggestions will be made that can be applied at the global level.

However, often a challenge we see is that organizations bring individuals in to try to fix the pistons without addressing the fact that you're out of fuel.

What we have seen clearly through speaking to and working with a range of organizations, is that HR and L&D work best when they are not a function, a department, in other words, separate. If you value your workforce then there is an awful lot that most organizations need to overhaul to really get that message across and put in place to enable them to do their best work. What constitutes HR varies a lot from organization to organization. As does what is the responsibility of HR, versus say the responsibility of a manager or the leadership team. It seems ludicrous to relegate all people matters to HR. People are often the core of an organization and subsequently everyone needs to understand and be responsible for creating optimal environments for them.

Here are some typical areas that normally come under the HR banner and some comments:

- Organization design: Any type of change management involved in redesigning an organization to be more fit for purpose will involve people and therefore it is useful to know what are some core behavioral and motivational drivers. It is also great to know how individuals could be supported in strengthening themselves so they can respond positively to change.
- Organization development: Anything that involves culture, values, enhancing performance, adaptability, and so on, benefits from understanding people. Helping to shape a workforce that is fit for the future can be done more efficiently and effectively when we understand how people change and what helps make them mentally fit. Something even as seemingly detached from people as strategy benefits from a deeper awareness of how people work, so the strategy can be going with the grain of people rather than against. It can also reduce the likelihood of undesirable side effects. If a strategy neglects some core human truths then it can cost an organization months or years in wasted efforts and outgoings.
- Resourcing and talent planning: Clearly identifying and attracting the right people for your organization is better done through understanding people. Similarly, strategizing and implementing ways to develop these people is enhanced through an understanding of neuroscience.

- Learning and development: Understanding how the brain learns impacts everything in L&D from strategy to implementation to evaluation. Previously we could only reverse engineer things, now with an enhanced understanding we can be more sophisticated in how we do things.
- Performance and reward: Reward is a big area of research in neuroscience and many of the insights are useful when we consider how we recognize and reward people. Working out how best to handle complex practices and having confidence in your decisions is easier if you know the science behind it.
- Employee engagement: Engaging people can be complex; however, neuroscience gives us insights into what is likely to produce better results. Our brain is where our emotional connection with work stems from. We can also learn from science how to communicate new ideas in a compelling way.
- Employee relations: Clarity, transparency, and certainty are things we know people benefit from, from a neuroscience perspective. Most organizations offer this through lots of policies and strategies. There may be another, more effective way.

Throughout this book several options are indirectly presented. The first is for you to keep things exactly as they are. You will have this additional information, process it, and may choose not to change a thing. The second option is to try to make some small changes. This is what most readers are likely to do. Many people feel constrained by their existing organizational set up, what the leaders do or don't buy into, and how things have always been done. The third option is to be bold.

Buurtzong, the health care organization in the Netherlands, has a revolutionary approach now. Their teams of 10–12 nurses do their own planning, they do holiday scheduling, administration, decide how many patients they will serve, their training needs and plans, whether to grow or split their team, how to monitor their performance, and what to do if productivity drops. They don't have an HR function. It is said that they give up economies of scale and gain unbridled motivation. EY examined

Buurtzong and found they require on average 40 percent fewer hours of care per client than other nursing organizations. (This is ironic when you learn about their approach, which involves them spending as much time with patients as they need, rather than having only 10 minutes allocated to bath someone.) Buurtzong patients stay in care only half as long, heal faster, and become more autonomous. The estimated savings for the Dutch social security system if all home care organizations achieved Buurtzong's results are close to 2 billion euros every year.

The numbers speak volumes. However, they don't tell of the restored joy a nurse gets from doing her job properly, from giving to her community in the way she knows is best. They don't mention the fact that the nurses are excited on Monday mornings and feel fulfilled on Friday afternoons. However, the fact that absenteeism for sickness is 60 percent lower and staff turnover is 33 percent lower than traditional nursing organizations does make most people sit up and take notice.[3]

ANDREA CARTWRIGHT – HR DIRECTOR, SUPERGROUP

Do I have to justify what I think will make an impact? Yes and no, if I want to go and spend some serious money on something then I'm going to have to justify it. But you know what? You can do an awful lot quite cheaply, what I call below the radar. [...] This is not a business that really instinctively gets HR [...] the chief exec certainly wouldn't. I remember sitting down with him at one point, taking him through my beautiful strategy that I'd written and he basically said, "I haven't got a clue what you are talking about," and I realized that we were going to need to approach this in a different way. So there is an element of [taking what] I call baby steps towards a vision that my team are already clear of but we don't ever talk about in the business because it's just too much to take people on board. What they can see is us getting stuff done and doing stuff to help them work more effectively, so that you get the definition and the reward in that respect, and of course the more you do that the more people are willing to go with the flow. Sometimes I do things and I beg for forgiveness afterwards.

Do HR Professionals Know This?

If the premise of this book is that neuroscience is important to HR and indeed the whole organization (which it is), then it makes sense to assess where the profession is at in terms of the perceived importance. I asked almost everyone I interviewed two final questions. The second, you will read about at the end of this book. The first was around whether they believed they were shaping people's brains. The responses were fascinating.

NEIL MORRISON – HR DIRECTOR, RANDOM HOUSE GROUP

So we have a mission that we want to help people to do the best work of their lives and that's what we are about. What that means is providing them with the security in the environment where they can really express themselves and perform. This doesn't mean that we drive their performance; it means we allow them to perform by not getting in the way of their performance. What I think we can do is we can help people to shape their own brains. If we are shaping their brains I think we've got a bit of a problem going on, but I think if we can create a place that stimulates, engages, and empowers them, then I think they will naturally grow and hopefully that will be them shaping their brains. Your expectations are driven by your experience; I think there will be times when we will get it wrong and we will create an experience that isn't wholly great for people and will maybe in some way damage their expectations in the future. In the same way that we say that we expect people to be able to make mistakes and learn, we've got to be able to make mistakes and learn as well, and sometimes we will get stuff wrong. [...] I would say that we are allowing them the space to shape it rather than we are doing it to [them].

DAVID JAMES – FORMER L&D DIRECTOR, DISNEY, FOUNDER OF WECOMMEND.COM

I think that we had loads of opportunities and tools to help shape people's brains. I personally think a 360 experience could be just ludicrously powerful. When you think, what a gift, that pretty much everybody who's got a decision in your career at one point is offering you feedback in such a positive light. The two verbatim "Please identify the strengths that help..." I don't remember the exact wording but then the developer one was: What if I change one thing? What would have the biggest impact on my performance? There was such wonderfully worded questions that the responses... I just thought it was absolute gold to provide somebody then with the opportunity to explore that, you've got two hours session, you'd explore it with them, immerse yourself into their world, you'd understand their context so that you could help them to have some real insights, so I think that is incredibly powerful. In that respect I'd say that we had opportunities to impact people.

I think that at a more junior level as well when people have first experience, communication models, that first point in which you realize, "Oh, wait a minute, I shouldn't speak to people how I wish to be spoken too; I should speak to them how *they* wish to be spoken to," and that is the first time that you recognize that you have a preference within a framework. I'm saying that any framework is better than no framework when you are first learning, so I think that exposure to all these wonderful models and tools [...] I think it's incredibly powerful and therefore I'm just a loud speaker for incredible content and that helps to shape people.

Part I
The Foundations

Part I is a series of introductions. You will meet the "Beautifully Simple Model that gets RESULTS," encounter the "Winning Scientific Formula," and learn how change really happens. We are laying foundations here. Ultimately you need a fundamental understanding of how people work and how the environment (internal and external) shapes how we work so you can make informed decisions. This may mean a transformational approach to your organization, or it may just mean making some tweaks.

You will learn that:

- Most organizations are just scratching the surface of what is possible
- Our brains are constantly being shaped
- You can change people's behaviors

If you are new to the brain then some of the terminology used in the book may sound alien. You have two choices: either head over to the book's website (www.engagedbrains.com) and take a quick crash course; alternatively replace any neuroscientific jargon with "the brain" as you read. This book is written specifically for people in organizations who are seeking a different lens that may help them experiment with looking at new and better ways forward; it isn't written for neuroscientists, but nor will the content be watered down.

The book speaks two further languages throughout it. The language of business that is prevalent in most organizations. It tends to be concerned with productivity, return on investment, and all the terms found in most business schools. The other language is more aligned with the next evolutionary wave of organizations that recognizes, for example, that trusting individuals means *really* trusting them. Not enabling them to act within tightly controlled and monitored parameters – but actually trusting them.

chapter **1**

The Beautifully Simple Model that Gets RESULTS

Results can be considered a consequence of behaviors. The way we behave is dependent on the internal environment of our brain and the external environment that we are in. In order to change our behaviors we can make informed changes to internal and external environments. These interactions are complex, however we can isolate and share some grounding principles taken from scientific research. For example, we know that sleep has a big impact on the internal environment of our brain. We know that a sleep-deprived person tends to behave in a different way, normally a less desirable way, and being sleep deprived makes it less likely you get the results you're looking for. However, many professional services organizations have a culture where going without sleep is a norm (Figure 1.1).

Results

Most organizations are looking for results. Results come in a huge variety of different shapes and sizes and can be measured or assessed in lots of different ways. Many organizations have challenges putting this beautifully simple model to work to get the results they are after. There are a few things worth being aware of. The brain likes to know what is expected of it. It likes there to be congruency between the different

FIGURE 1.1 / The beautifully simple model that gets RESULTS

ways it is being communicated to. If we are getting mixed messages then we can become distrustful of our organization. This can have a negative impact on many areas of business and individuals.

So the first thing to do is to get crystal clear on the results you are looking to achieve. We're talking about a high level of specificity around what "great" would look like. This is an organization-wide objective. If you have HR saying one thing, leadership saying another, PR saying yet another, and the promotion policy reflecting something else, then whatever a person does could be perceived as wrong. Let's have a look at an area of the brain that gets activated when there are mixed messages coming through and a lack of clarity around what we're supposed to be doing. (Whenever areas of the brain are mentioned in this book you may choose to dive in and soak up everything you can or you may choose to skim over some bits.)

THE INSULA

If we do something that we process as an error then it is useful to us to be aware of this so we can make strategic behavioral and neuronal adjustments.[1] Error awareness is our ability to perceive our own mistakes. When we fail to achieve the intended outcome from an action we detect this. Errors can be costly at the time or in the future. In neuroscience straight-forward simple error detection is studied, because it gets very complex as we add more variables. The part of the brain called the insula is involved in the process of us becoming aware of errors. It is not yet clear whether we need to be consciously aware of errors in order to make post-error adjustments.[2] While the anterior insula appears to be the most important part of the brain for error detection the posterior medial frontal cortex and the thalamus also are of relevance. We know that the insula is also important for interoception.[3, 4]

When errors are detected they can trigger autonomic responses such as a change in heart rate and skin conductance. This could potentially be detected by the insula. This would link interoception to error detection. As the brain processes interoceptive information it may deliver that information to support error awareness. It has been proposed that the insula could act like a relay station in regulating interactions between our brain networks that are involved in external attention and interoceptive cognition.[5] The insula may be considered as part of an attentional network. It is involved in processing unexpected outcomes[6] and increased necessity of effort.[7, 8]

Our attention is a precious commodity. It is linked to our productivity, the quality of our thinking, our creativity, and much more. It is mentally tiring to have to constantly evaluate whether something is the desired result or whether we should be doing something else.

Things also get complicated when we don't really know what the intended outcome from our action should be. Imagine an employee who is given the goal from his manager of getting as much cash in this month as possible. On the wall in front of him are the company's values, which include honesty and trustworthiness. In addition he is incentivized to reach a certain number of appointments each week. Is his goal to maximize profit from this interaction, be honest and trustworthy, or deliver the quickest service possible? By having competing objectives he is going to fail in some respect whatever he does. His brain will register this.

Challenges

The way we communicate what we're looking for from our employees encompasses many different approaches. Unfortunately, organizations can confuse their people about the results that they are looking for from them. They are sent mixed messages. Often individuals or whole departments work independently from each other. They may have been trained in a particular way or may have picked up common practices from other organizations. Just because you've been told by an accredited training company or your last employer to do something a certain way doesn't mean it is the best way forward. (Of course it may be ... but there will be other factors.)

Imagine a scenario where your head of learning and development (L&D) has heard about the 70:20:10 theory.[9] They think the idea of a reference model that values learning within the workflow and social learning[10] is fantastic. They want to "implement it." They stop investing in the traditional training sessions that have been commonplace in the organization. Instead they put up some posters encouraging people to "live and learn." There are already many modules available on the online learning platform that people can take at their leisure.

Unfortunately, this particular organization's culture values the billable hours people clock up. In addition, bonuses paid are linked to achieving objectives set at the start of the year. These don't mention learning at all.

Overcoming the Challenges

Sometimes even simple models can be deceptively hard to implement. Walking into many organizations today, as we do, we would agree. Things are often not set up to make it easy for employees. The brain loves to conserve energy where it can, so we need to try to make it easy. In order to cultivate certain behaviors from people, we want to consider the environment that they exist within. In this chapter, we introduce the fundamentals so that you will notice the underlying concepts running throughout the rest of the book. We go into more depth on the internal environment in Chapter 5, The Jarring Awakening, and on the external environment in Part IV.

Behavior: Clarify, Design, Shape

Everything in this book concerns influencing behavior. There is, of course, the question of whether we should be shaping people's behaviors. The reality is that organizations are shaping behaviors, and the question remains whether they are doing it intentionally and in alignment with who the organization is.

Often the approach is haphazard, and the end result leaves a lot to be desired. It is really important that when considering behavior change you start at the beginning and CLARIFY the results you really want. You need to be crystal clear on what you are actually looking for, and the level of detail you need here is far greater than most people realize. Next, you need to identify the behaviors that will generate those results. The following step is to DESIGN, ideally based on existing research data, the internal and external environments that will help those behaviors be most likely. The final implementation stage is to SHAPE those environments to do their job. It is a simple, but thorough approach. It takes time to do it properly and is in some ways a lifelong project.

Environment

When I ask you what environment your colleagues are making decisions in, what normally springs to mind? Most people's thoughts go straight to their external environment, their office perhaps. This is a powerful environment, but one could argue that the internal environment – the brain and mind – are even more persuasive.

External Environment

It is in Part IV where we really explore the potential for our different environments and the effects they can have on how we work. While writing this book I was privileged to explore lots of different workplaces. Most organizations have spaces that they believe are practical. I would challenge what the purpose of the space is. If you could increase one person's productivity by 10 percent, what impact would that have? Would it be worth losing space for three people? Before you dismiss any changes as unrealistic or not for you wait until Part IV, where we explore the impact the spaces we work in can have on us. In this section, let us just start to see what others have done.

Many organizations are thinking outside the box:

At Pixar they have a little row of huts, like beach huts crossed with really nice sheds, each of which is an office. There are balls of fairy lights hanging from the ceiling, giving it an outdoor feel. The walls are blue, and there are comfy sofas for waiting or thinking on. In another area, there are structures that could have originated as normal rooms that have a big oval hole cut out of the wall as the entrance space. Inside hang retro orange glow lanterns. On the floor is a chaise longue, above that a large mirror. In the corner, a raised workstation with computer screens. The feel is chic retro (from my perspective) and is hugely novel and stimulating.

Red Bull in London is very different. It is shiny ... like an office from the future. The reception desk has thick silver metal sheets framing the simple white desk. There are unusually shaped red, green, and black chairs in areas throughout the building. Glass barriers stop people falling from floor to floor. The stairs look a bit like vacuum cleaner ends, but you may choose to use the huge white slide to travel down a floor. One meeting room even has a round table set with six chairs with a ping-pong net through the middle.

Mindlab in Copenhagen know what they are doing. One space is an egg-shaped meeting room in which all the walls are whiteboards. Once you're in you can write on any of the surfaces.

What If? Innovation have been named the UK's happiest workplace in the past. The space works for them. Reception doubles up as a meeting space, which is a hub for the team. There are comments of praise written in this area on the walls and ceiling, naming employees and sharing specific examples of greatness. Often we see slightly (or very) odd things in workplaces. Here you'll meet a cow in a Spiderman outfit.

Budget obviously becomes a factor at some point. But for just a little bit more let's expand our thinking. At Inventionland in Pittsburgh, they have an amazing indoor tree house. There is greenery above and water below. A tire swing hangs from one side, and a balcony area gives a great view. Over the other side of the office is a pirate ship complete with shark-infested waters.

At TBWA Hakuhodo in Tokyo there are areas of grass where people can sit and work.

Google, perhaps unsurprisingly, have a range features in their different offices. You can find a large hammock – where lots of people could all sit/lie at once, lots of interesting pod-type meeting rooms in a variety of different styles; pods with cushions inside and trees outside, low-level lighting, and a fireman's pole; beach bars, pinball machines, and pool tables; and massage areas (that look like a little spa), exercise rooms, and of course meditation rooms with chairs you can recline and aquariums.

The Cath Kidson offices in London look just as you would expect them to. They are filled everywhere with the beautiful design prints. There is a lovely cafe that is top-to-toe in the identifiable brand. It is also a truly practical space, it has lovely looking food and drink and it really draws people in. Subsequently lots of meetings happen there, over a cup of tea. It has got that creative feel and would certainly appeal to the fans of the product who work there.

LOUISA FRYER – L&D MANAGER
CATH KIDSON

Yes, so this is how it works. We usually get very busy at lunch time and then we also sometimes have like ... so when we have our inductions the starters would be sitting together and we also do our monthly updates in here and we've also got a place

> downstairs. This building is quite good, we've got this space, we've got the mock shop, we've got the ground floor showroom, which is massive, and that is where all the product goes for international partners, where they could come and have a look at the product, but that is another space where we all get together.

The mock shop is exactly as it sounds. An average-sized shop where everything from shop displays to customer service training can be tested out – a fantastic idea.

The reason for sharing these examples is not to say you have to be incorporating all these ideas ... far from it, in fact. Start by clarifying what behaviors you want (ensuring those selected will get you the results you desire). Then design the external environment that can help you facilitate those behaviors. Finally shape the environment. Jumping straight to "a slide is such a cool idea – let's get one installed here" misses a big part of the process. Although, on the flip side, if the idea of a slide is really exciting and motivating to you, then perhaps it would be a good idea.

Internal Environment

What shapes our internal environment? So much that it is exciting and a little scary. We have the scope here to start the discovery, and the most important thing you can take from this piece is to be intentional in your shaping.

be intentional in your shaping

Do our genes matter?

Absolutely. One study examined the success traders experienced on Wall Street. There are some technical terms mentioned in what follows, you may choose to follow along, looking up any new terms, or digest the summary. The researchers looked at the genes that affect dopamine levels and the career tenure of professional traders. A group of traders were genotyped and compared to a control group of people who did not trade stocks. It was found that distinct alleles of the dopamine receptor 4 promoter and catecholamine-O-methyltransferase were predominant in the traders. These alleles affect synaptic dopamine and are associated with moderate levels of the neurotransmitter, rather than very high or very low levels. Here is where it gets super interesting for us. *The activity of the alleles correlated positively with the number of years spent trading at Wall Street.* Also differences in personality and trading behavior were correlated with the allelic variants. This brings together the links between our genes, our behaviors, our traits, and our success.[11] In summary, it appears that the longer a person spent on Wall Street the more predominant a gene that affects dopamine was likely to be. This also was linked to how the traders behaved.

You may have been brought up thinking that genes are more fixed than perhaps we believe them to be now. When sharing this piece of research with my husband and mother over Sunday lunch the response was a little skeptical. If things conflict with your previous understanding, try to remember that it may have been a while since you last studied the basics, and indeed the experts are working five days a week on these topics. If initially something doesn't sit right it may not be because it is wrong, it may be because we need to upgrade the information in our brain against which we are evaluating. That said, the expression of different genes can be affected by our behaviors. Let's look at an example from meditators.

A group of experienced meditators were asked to engage in mindful practice for eight hours. They were compared to a control group of untrained individuals, who engaged in quiet non-meditative activities. The meditators showed a range of genetic and molecular differences. These changes included altered levels of gene regulating machinery and reduced levels of proinflammatory genes. This means that gene expression can alter rapidly.[12] One of the authors of the study, Davidson, said "Our genes are quite dynamic in their expression and these results suggest that the calmness of our mind can actually have a potential influence on their expression." With this being proved to have an effect on our genetic expression, imagine what else is affecting us daily.

It's all in the mind

Recently a study was done on trust. First the participants filled out a questionnaire about their own tendency to trust others. They also looked at pictures of neutral faces, and were asked to rate how trustworthy they thought each person was. This gave the researchers an indication of how trusting the participant was of others. MRI (magnetic resonance imaging) scans were also taken of the participants. Haas said,

> The most important finding was that the grey matter volume was greater in the ventral medial prefrontal cortex, which is the brain region that serves to evaluate social rewards, in people that tended to be more trusting of others [...] Another finding that we observed was for a brain region called the amygdala. The volume of this area of the brain, which codes for emotional saliency, was greater in those that were both most trusting and least trusting of others. If something is emotionally important to us, the amygdala helps us code and remember it.[13]

Moving from trust to generosity to further explore the internal environment, let's have a look at the hormone and neuromodulator oxytocin (OT). Most people would think of generosity as a trait, describing friends or colleagues as generous in a favorable way. Interestingly, the behavior of being generous is easier to influence than perhaps many would have thought. In one study participants were infused with OT and then asked how they would split a sum of money with a stranger. The control group was not given any OT, but was given a placebo instead. Those with the extra OT were 80 percent more generous than the placebo group.[14]

On the flip side, the hormone testosterone decreases generosity. In another study testosterone was given to 15 men to see what impact it had on prosocial behaviors. The "ultimatum" game was then played and it was found that those with raised testosterone were 27 percent. It was also noted that men with elevated testosterone were more likely to use their money to punish those who were ungenerous towards them. The authors of this study concluded that elevated testosterone causes men to behave antisocially.[15]

The intention of this section is simply to introduce you to the reality that our internal environment, focusing in this book on our brain, has a powerful effect on our behavior. It makes total logical sense when people think about it. The extension from that, though, is that we're only relatively recently able to grasp, from an evidence-based standpoint, what is going on in that internal environment. There is often a delay getting new information out there and into the hands of people who can do something with it. This book is intended to give decision-makers an evidence base from which to do things differently: namely, to value and give resources to the shaping of the internal environment.

value and give resources to the shaping of the internal environment

Does everything have to happen in a lab?

Of course not! Labs are great places to do experiments to collect data. However the practical applications can be seen in the workplace. Amy Cuddy has become quite famous after she shared her research into power poses in her TED talk. Her team set out to identify the mechanism through which power posing could improve performance. They looked at speed quality (intelligent, clear, and well structured) and presentation quality (enthusiastic, confident, and captivating). From previous research they knew that power reduces stress, anxiety, and negative effect, which they presumed would make individuals more confident, captivating, and enthusiastic.[16] Creating an internal environment rich in testosterone and low in cortisol can be done using power poses.[17]

Realizing the close relationship between what we think and do and how our internal environment actually physically changes as a result can be empowering. We can make more informed choices.

This chapter has been introductory in nature. It is being brought to a close with something really practical, powerful, and possible. It is also very simple, it demonstrates one of the instances where the latest brain research underpins and strengthens the old experience-based advice that has been given for decades.

Sleep

When did we start thinking it was okay to work instead of sleep? How did this pathological acceptance start? Was it from our desire to *achieve* more? We have been measuring success based on what we *accomplish*. The things we measure tend to be linked to classic productivity. For a lawyer it would be things like how many billable hours they are able to charge. In order to increase our productivity, and subsequently how "successful" we are perceived as being, we seem to have stumbled upon the idea of reducing our sleep. So does this lead to real organizational success?

The research suggests not. Your experience can probably help you get a feel for this too. Cast your mind back, perhaps not too far, to the morning after a late night. How did you feel when your alarm went off? Did you wish you could hit snooze? Eyes feel a little heavier than normal? Head feel a little foggy?

In this section many different compelling arguments for getting at least enough sleep are presented. The reason for this is because many organizations are not yet paying attention to this valuable results-influencing tool. It may not be sexy or cutting edge or new, but the fact that it, in all its simplicity, is not yet being fully listened to and acted upon means it warrants further attention.

What Are the Benefits of Sleep?

We know that not getting enough sleep can lead to poorer cognitive performance and altered emotional functioning. What happens when we get *more* than enough sleep? Is it worth doing or a lazy unproductive use of time? A study that looked at this "sleep credit" (getting more sleep than one subjectively requires) found a correlation in those habitually sleeping more and those with greater gray matter volumes within the left medial prefrontal cortex and right orbitofrontal gyrus. Building up a sleep "credit" also correlated with having greater emotional intelligence and better mental health.[18] This is a long-term investment you're making by habitually getting more sleep than you "need."

Now we shall take a look at how investing in sleep can deliver a quick return. Would solving problems more quickly be valuable to you? Or an organization where people had insights into how to do things better? If so, encouraging a culture that values sleep appears to be a good move. An "insight" has long been understood to involve a mental restructuring that leads to a sudden gain of explicit knowledge, which allows qualitatively changed behavior. (Bit of a mouthful, but you've almost certainly experienced that flash of realization when you see something clearly that was shadowed or completely hidden before.) Researchers asked the participants of their study to perform a cognitive task that required them to learn some stimulus–response sequences. They improved gradually by increasing response speed across task blocks. There was also the opportunity to improve abruptly after gaining insight into a hidden abstract rule underlying all sequences.[19]

Initially everyone went through training to establish a task representation. Then participants enjoyed eight hours of either nocturnal sleep, nocturnal wakefulness (not so enjoyable) or daytime wakefulness. They were then retested, and more than twice as many participants had gained insight into the hidden rule after sleep as after being awake (regardless of whether than was during the night or day). The researchers concluded "that sleep, by restructuring new memory representations, facilitates extraction of explicit knowledge and insightful behaviour."

One of the most well-known roles of sleep is around memory reactivation and consolidation. It is believed that declarative memories change after the initial learning episode due to the formation and interaction with other memories. This means that we can develop complex networks of interrelated memories, align memories with long-term strategies and goals, and generate insights based on novel combinations of these memory fragments.[20]

The neurophysiology of how memories are consolidated during sleep is fascinating, but details of this are perhaps beyond what we need from a practical perspective. It is important to note, however, that sleep patterns in the limbic system are essential for the preservation of experience-induced synaptic modifications.[21] Without synaptic plasticity we would be pretty stuck.

What Happens If You Don't Get Enough Sleep?

There is some research that a lack of sleep has further interesting, and undesirable, affects. Michael Christian and Aleksander Ellis looked at what happened when people were suffering from sleep deprivation. They found that along with the predictable decrease in productivity, loss of self-control, lowered ability to regulate thoughts, emotions, and behaviors, and feelings of hostility, there was another interesting finding. People were engaging in workplace deviance. Examples included falsifying receipts for reimbursement, working slower in order to earn more overtime pay, using drugs or alcohol while at work, and criticizing or verbally degrading colleagues.

When researchers probed further and provided students with an incentive to steal answers to a test, they discovered a fascinating trend. More of the sleep-deprived students stole the answers than their adequately rested peers. It is understood that sleep deprivation decreases brain function in the prefrontal cortex. This is akin to our boss, who is responsible for executive functioning, coming into work a bit drunk. The ability to control emotions or govern behaviors is impaired. When someone has had less sleep than they need, their self-regulation is decreased. This is an undesirable state to be in.

One of the most concerning aspects about this research is that our experience of speaking with organizations mirrors what Ellis has voiced, "In fact, in certain industries, lack of sleep is worn as a badge of honour."

So What Else Does Sleep Do?

When we sleep our brain is working a little like a dishwasher, cleaning out harmful toxins that have built up. By clearing them out we may be reducing our risk of Alzheimer's. Fascinating research done with mice showed the lymphatic system opening up and allowing cerebrospinal fluid to flow rapidly through the brain during sleep. When the mice were awake this system prevented most of the flow. Measurements suggest that the spaces between our brain cells may increase when we sleep, enabling the brain to flush though the toxins. Dr. Maiken Nedergaard, a leader of the study, said, "Sleep changes the cellular structure of the brain. It appears to be a completely different state."[22] Experientially this makes sense. Historically sleep is something that our ancestors have been doing for as far back as we can trace. Scientifically we don't yet have the full picture around sleep, but everything we do have leads us to the practical conclusion that it is a good thing to value and prioritize doing.

The Modern Antidote?

Many people use caffeine to delay the negative effects of sleep deprivation. We may feel it helps us to keep going or to focus. One recent study showed that people who had been kept awake overnight and then given caffeine were less likely to "cut ethical corners at work" by lying to earn extra money in a situation designed to emulate a work environment. The participants of the study who had not received the caffeine after their night being kept awake were more willing to participate in these undesirable behaviors.[23] Does this mean that organizations should provide caffeine in the workplace? We would prefer some of the other suggestions these researchers made including:

• Reducing the long hours people are expected to work
• Providing workplace napping facilities and sleep awareness training
• Avoiding doing tasks that require high levels of self-control when you expect to be sleep deprived.

A recent study showed that consuming caffeine even six hours before going to bed can have disruptive effects on both objective and subjective measures of sleep.[24] These results give a scientific underpinning to the sleep hygiene recommendation of avoiding caffeine in the afternoon.

How Does Caffeine Work?

This is one of the times where understanding what is actually going on when you down a cup of coffee can be useful. With this knowledge you may still choose to consume caffeine, but you may do so more strategically, knowing the likely future symptoms. So, as you go through the day the neurochemical adenosine is released and levels build up. Your nervous system monitors these levels and passes through receptors, which makes you feel sleepy. We talk about receptors as working like a lock-and-key mechanism. Following this analogy through, caffeine is the same size and shape as adenosine so can also fit the receptor lock, also known as the A1 receptor. While the caffeine occupies the receptors, adenosine cannot, so even while the adenosine is building up, you don't feel tired. Alongside this process your dopamine levels are increasing which gives you that boost.

Once the caffeine wears off, the build-up of adenosine needs to be processed by the receptors – this takes time and can leave you feeling groggier than before you started on the coffee.

Caveat Around the Beautifully Simple Model

As is often the case, when you simplify something down you can lose some truth. The model may be useful, but may not be the whole story. In this case it is believed that more than just behaviors influence a result. However, in most organizations beginning with aligning behaviors is a great place to start.

What's the Bottom Line?

Key take aways from the Beautifully Simple Model that gets RESULTS

- Get clear on what results your organization cannot compromise.
- Map out the behaviors needed to achieve those results and check that they don't clash.
- Create the environment to support those behaviors.

What Can I Do Today?

Choose one result that you want to focus on. CLARIFY the behaviors that would enable you to achieve the result. Then DESIGN the internal and external environments that would best support you. Finally take your first steps to SHAPE them.

What Can I Put in Place for the Long Term?

Quarterly meetings where different departments ensure the expected behaviors are aligned and will deliver the results.

Quarterly design-thinking sessions that explore what internal and external environments would best support people to achieve the desired behaviors.

What Is the Overall Ideal Vision?

An organization that invests in both the internal and external environment of its employees.

chapter 2

Introducing the Winning Scientific Formula

Key Takeaways

- Invest most of your time, energy and other resources into engaging people.
- Understand how people are motivated and proactively minimize any demotivation.
- Utilize systems to manage behaviors.

Introducing the Winning Scientific Formula

The brain likes things simple. It is easy to over complicate things; indeed layers of complexity are sometimes useful. However initially it can pay to start simple. Many problems arise in organizations because people are not engaged, motivated, and managed effectively. In our mission to see people excited on Mondays and fulfilled on Fridays, this simple approach is hugely powerful (Figure 2.1).

Each of these simple components has complex neural correlates – what is going on in the brain. In the past we have tried to get people engaged, motivated, or managed in a particular way without really understanding

FIGURE 2.1 / The winning scientific formula

what is going on inside people's heads. Watching people is great, but it misses out an important part of the story. This book is dedicated to unveiling and telling that part of the story.

Let's flesh it out a little. You want to start by engaging people. Pour most of your time, energy, and resources into making it easy for people to engage. The process of increasing engagement is not typically done overnight (although specific interventions *can* make a difference that quickly, and last). It can be useful to consider this a journey with great landmarks on the way.

Why Would We Want to Engage People?

According to *The Evidence*, a report collated in collaboration with University of Bath School of Management:[1]

- Organizations with high employee engagement levels outperform low engagement counterparts in both total shareholder returns and higher annual net income.
- Organizations with high and sustainable engagement levels enjoyed an average one-year operating margin that was almost three times higher than the lower engagement organizations.
- Marks & Spencer found that over a four-year period their stores with improving engagement had delivered on average £62 million more sales than those with declining engagement.
- 85 percent of the world's most admired companies believe that their efforts to engage their employees have reduced employee performance problems.

- Higher engagement scores are correlated with higher productivity.
- Quality errors in a manufacturing company were lower in more engaged teams.
- More engagement is linked to better understanding of customer needs.
- There is a longitudinal relationship between engagement and the Net Promoter Score.
- Patient satisfaction is significantly higher in the NHS trusts that benefit from higher engagement.
- Engaged people are more likely to say that work brings out their most creative ideas.
- Encouraging shop floor input at BAE plus encouraging more engagement reduced time taken to build planes by 25 percent.
- Disengaged employees take an average of 6.19 days off while engaged employees average 2.69 days off due to sickness.
- Engagement leads to lower turnover rates.
- Lower engagement correlates with poorer health and safety.

Do I have even more of your attention now? The business case for engagement is strong. It makes sense to understand as much as possible about how to engage people because it will have a positive impact on the organization, as well as the individual.

The Neuroscience of Engagement

Dopamine, serotonin, oxytocin, epinephrine, norepinephrine, and other chemicals all can play their part in helping a person be engaged. Every area of the brain you have heard of is also likely to be involved in engagement at one stage or another. Having assimilated a lot of the research and looked at a lot of organizations, I would suggest that there are many neural routes to engaging an individual. The aim would be for organizations to cover the basics, as covered in Part II, and use the management insights from Part IV to help people strengthen the neural circuits of engagement. This would mean that even during the tough times at work they wouldn't become fully disengaged. The pull of the engagement set up from the concepts in Part II should lay down the foundations with their chosen place of work to the degree that affords them, and the organization, some resilience.

Every organization is at a different stage of their journey. Ideas you may encounter in this book may be a little down the line from where you are currently or you may be looking to tackle some big changes (in which case, keep reading). Martin shares where they focused when he started with a city council.

MARTIN GLOVER - HEAD OF HR BUSINESS PARTNERSHIP & TRANSFORMATIONAL CHANGE, CITY OF EDINBURGH COUNCIL

How do we engage people? I think we're learning all the time. When I joined the council my background had mostly been in the private sector. There was a sense that employee engagement didn't really happen. We're still tussling with this. We set up the architecture, defining what employee engagement is and then what the systems and processes are that we can recognize it, do it, and tell the story of it. We have an employee engagement forum, led by the HR director. We were talking about that the normal conversations around change that happen daily, and the idea we came up with is employee engagement. We need to be able to tell that story. Not just about the impact it has on people at work but those who are on the receiving end of our services.

Communications

1. How do we get the story and tell the story?
2. How do we measure that through the various surveys and instruments we use?
3. How do we embed that within the organization and how do we get acknowledgement for that?
4. What are the tools, tips, and hints that we can give to managers to help with their people?

Are You Engaged Yet?

Shawn Achor suggests that the current paradigm that most people subscribe to (consciously or otherwise), that is, that they need to work hard
in order to be successful in order to be happier or feel more engaged and
fulfilled at work, is flawed and that the formula needs to be flipped on
its head. The reality is that both scenarios and orders of things can work.
Being engaged does release dopamine and serotonin, which can make
you want to work harder and subsequently be more successful. Working
hard and recognizing the goals you are achieving can also release dopamine and serotonin. Many people only focus on the huge goals – like a
promotion or a high salary – and then miss out on the boost effect all the
small achievements could offer along the way. If you move the goal post
as soon as you get close, then you may not feel happy or want to keep
going.[2] You're not training yourself to see that hard work is rewarding.

HESKETH – NHS PROPERTY SERVICES

One of our business objectives is to become employer of
choice, which I know sounds fabulous and everybody says that
sort of stuff and you will see annual reports that say people are
our most important asset, but what I like and why I'm personally
committed to the job I'm doing is because I see that the organization as a whole is genuinely wanting to do the right thing
with people. I think there is a genuine interest because there is a
recognition that, ultimately, engagement leads to more contribution, enjoyment, and everything being positive.

Opportunities to engage staff are often hidden in plain sight. Of course
some of the most powerful ways to engage the people who work with
you involve engaging the people who are most important to them; their
families.

HESKETH – NHS PROPERTY SERVICES

We'd spoken to the unions about the weekly to monthly pay and they developed, on our behalf, a package of training and supports for the staff, which we offered nationally. Then I had a union member say to me that traditionally it's not always the wage earner that is the budget holder of the house, what about allowing spouses or significant others to come to the training, and I immediately said yes and the unions said, "What?," I said, "Why wouldn't we?" It's going to cost us a bit more money possibly, because we are going to have a few more people but that's for the teas, coffees, and staff, and if we are driven by "we want to do this to support people in being successful," why wouldn't you do something that you would think would help make it successful? But what I find weird is that [...] you come to the work place and suddenly you can't do things that are bloody obvious. I think we had only one or two partners come but the other benefit of that is we are seen to offer it as well, so whether it is used, or not, I think it's all part of the whole picture.

Why Motivation?

Today it is fairly acceptable for people to talk about people needing to be motivated to do something. That wasn't necessarily always the case though. The "carrot and stick" approach is still systematically endorsed in many organizations with a heavy dose of monitoring often present. This tends to be focused around the external environment. So, increasing people's pay or giving them a bonus to reward the type of behavior we want to see more of; disciplining people, giving verbal or written warnings if things escalate, to punish behavior we want to see less of.

Essentially we need to flip the motivation approach on its head. Rather than it being something we struggle to do once people are disengaged and demotivated, it needs to be considered ahead of time. The culture should be a motivating one. The practices and systems should be rewarding rather than threatening.

The Neuroscience of Motivation

When we think about motivation we want to really focus in on the reward networks. This means looking at midbrain dopamine and its targets in reward prediction. Our brain cleverly, through dopamine neurons, signals a reward prediction error to enable us to predict and act to increase the probability of reward in the future. This process accounts for the reinforcement learning that we see.[3] When people come into organizations and are engaged and motivated the opportunity is to prove that the individual's expectations were right: that working here *will* be rewarding. Their reward network should be firing regularly and cementing in for them that they made a great decision.

individual's expectations
were right: that working
here will be rewarding

Another area to consider, when thinking about motivation, is the relationship between goal-directed and habitual behaviors. While more research is ongoing in this area, current thinking centers around the prefrontal cortex's involvement in goal-directed behavior. Historically, habitual behaviors have implicated the striatum. It is looking more probable that both categories of behavior in fact implicate a distinct corticostriatal loop involving parts of both the prefrontal cortex and the striatum.[4, 5]

It is worth bearing in mind that when organizations tend to think, "Right, we need to motivate these guys," it is often at a time that it will be quite difficult to make a significant difference. A big part of motivation happens under the radar using parts of the hot network. Remember, the time to invest in strengthening things is now. The longer things are left, the more work it becomes to change. From the first interaction a person has with an organization, your opportunities begin to layer-in positive memories about it. These can be drawn upon to motivate behaviors down the road.

Why Management?

On the radio the other day there was a study being shared. It was one of the pieces of research that showed that when people are given smaller plates they tend to eat less. There is such a great selection of research now out there that show the amazing effects that our external environment can have on our behavior, it is wonderful. During our partnership with the Wales Centre for Behaviour Change at Bangor University, an experiment was done that nudged people into taking the stairs instead of the lift or elevator, just by strategically placing a sticker over a floor tile. The simplicity of these interventions often challenges people.

The radio presenters, as often happens, were disagreeing with the study, "No, I just don't buy it," one said, "if I want to eat less I will. I don't need a plate to tell me what to do." They had missed several of the points.

Anyone whose role seeks to manage the behavior of people should realize how complex what they are trying to do could be and that there are often different ways to create a solution that meets your real goal. Let's imagine you are responsible for managing baggage handlers. You are getting a lot of complaints from customers that they have to wait for their bags. Old-school management theories might take you straight to thoughts of rewarding desirable behavior. Suppose you were to decide to financially incentivize the handlers to get the first bag onto the belt within a certain time frame, say 10 minutes after the plane docks. What may happen (indeed it has in the past) is that they do absolutely get *the first bag* onto the belt within that time frame. They even get the second and third on. However, then they go onto the next plane and belt so they can receive the next bonus. You still end up with complaining customers. Suppose next you employed more baggage handlers so more hands would make lighter (speedier) work. Well, Houston airport did just this, and yet they still got complaints.[6]

Sometimes there are other ways to achieve the outcome you're looking for. In this instance, they moved the arrival gates further from the baggage carousel, meaning that when people arrived their baggage was normally there already and they were pleasantly surprised.

What Is the Neuroscience of Management?

Much of what goes on in the sophisticated management of environments, systems, and anything that can influence people's behavior utilizes the hot network rather than the cold. So rather than the old-school approach of "just tell people what you need them to do," there are a host of ways you can tell parts of their brain that operate without the consciousness needing to be involved.

One of our most powerful drivers is our connec-tion to other people as we see in Chapter 6, "The Reassuring Truth." If relationships are strong then you can achieve a lot.

If relationships are strong then you can achieve a lot

NEIL MORRISON – HR DIRECTOR, RANDOM HOUSE GROUP

I bang on time and time again saying "people do things for peo-ple," they don't do things for processes or policies. If you want to change behavior you need to interact on a human-to-human level. Too many organizations and leadership teams try to change behavior through policies and processes and procedures. And that doesn't change anything. It may modify it slightly for a time. If you build a park, ultimately you'd be better off not putting footpaths down until you see where people actually walk. That for me is the way in which human-focused organizations manage by understanding human behavior at a person-to-person level. Rather than trying to define behavior by corporate structure.

Neil insightfully shares from an experiential perspective why we place man-agement last in the formula. It is important, and policies, processes and proce-dures all can be incredibly useful, however *real organizational success* doesn't use them to replace engagement. There are also a host of organizations that use comparatively few of the traditional management systems, we would suggest that the management is happening in a very different way.

LOUISA FRYER – L&D MANAGER, CATH KIDSON

I think things happen very quickly and some things that get through or some things get missed; induction was probably one the biggest things that was missed. There was nothing here. You have to think about the people working here and you have to make it visual engaging, interesting, compelling. I didn't want to go with a heavy, traditional approach to something, without the technology I needed. I need it to be really colorful and I would really like to have some technology to support on-boarding – improving toward that would be great.

We are talking about the culture and what it's actually like to work here, what you can experience in this size and scale, and [to] get [across] a tone of the business, so we've written these welcome magazines and it is really good because it's that dwell time before handing in the notice and starting at the new company, that is the most engaged point. So that magazine is for that period of time: it's to help engage people and help them get excited about what they are coming to or for the store manager to give it to the girl before her first shift and she can read it, and then there are some bits and pieces that, later down the line, show whether you are ready or not. So [a] subtle kind of teasing and learning from that early stage. I'm proud of that because I think that is really important, that has really stayed with me when I learned about that engage point, before we could actually get here, is the most engaged.

So now the right start induction, basically we've set it up so that if you come in to store you have an experience, we are trying to keep the content the same but it's delivered in chunks depending on where you are and to suit the environment you are coming into. So if you are a manager starting in the business, you will come for a two-day induction here, and the induction consists of stuff around the print, around sales, around the product, and around the brand. Then if you join a store you get the same content, but delivered in more bite-sized chunks. It's all over the internet, the manager will deliver it through and they will submit tours and have bits and pieces that they get as well, and they would also get their new program folder, which is called e-competencies, and they start working through that. So that is how it works.

"How would you like to be managed?" That was the first time I'd ever asked that question and it was because I knew that he was very mature within his role; I knew that technically I didn't want to interfere with what he was doing, I know that I've got a great deal of experience and I'd crossed his path a little bit but who I am to tell him what to do? In fact, I gave him two territories to grow and explore, so it was a case of I know you can do the job what would you like from me? And at the time it kind of amazed him, so I just said, "Well you should think about that, I want to talk about it next time." So I gave him the job and we talked about it afterwards and I think that he said that he wants to be created within the role, I said, "OK, so that's not for me to confine, so maybe I'm more about asking questions and prompting you to think bigger." There were things that I needed him to do, so I would push him on certain things, but other than that I've just held him to account.

What's the Bottom Line?

You need to engage, motivate, and manage effectively. That order and proportion of energy investment is wise.

What Can I Do Today?

Today and every day to increase positivity and engagement:

1. Write down three new things you are grateful for linked to your work.
2. Write down the impact your work may have had on someone.
3. Meditate at some point at work; it can be for two minutes or five minutes or, if you're feeling really generous with yourself, even longer!

4. Take some exercise during the day – run up and down the stairs 10 times, go for a walk, do a couple of yoga poses – get moving.
5. Thank or praise someone specifically every day.

Encourage any teams you work with to trial these strategies too and see how they feel after two weeks and then four weeks.

Increase your awareness around how you motivate and manage. Are you clear on what activates people's reward networks and threat response? Do you capitalize on the external environment and systems to manage?

What Can I Put in Place for the Long Term?

Create a "Engagement Coaches Club." Start by inviting people to apply to become an Engagement Coach. The first stage of the role involves proactively increasing their knowledge around engagement. The second stage is to gather some data and look at where engagement is at currently. (This may need to be done in collaboration with HR or other departments.) The third stage is to utilize design thinking approaches to explore what could increase engagement across the organization. A "no stone left unturned" approach is best. It could be very useful to engage people from different teams in this exploration stage. The fourth stage is to coach stakeholders. Partner with them to explore what they think and how they want to move things forward. The fifth stage is to support with implementation as needed. Then the next year the whole cycle is repeated.

What Is the Overall Ideal Vision?

An organization that believes it leads people and manages things and that the organization is a body that the right people love being engaged with.

3

How Change Really Happens

Key Takeaways

- What people repeatedly do, think, or experience will make it more likely they do that again.
- Attention is valuable – think about where you direct it.
- You have a responsibility, an opportunity, beyond office hours.

Introduction

If you are toying with the possibility of wanting to get better results in your organization then this is a key chapter for understanding the theory behind *how* to do that. Why do we bother with theory? We believe that by understanding *how* something works then we have flexibility in creating solution-focused approaches. Essentially, if you're looking for results to be different (any results) then you'll need people to behave differently. These behaviors are typically a result of a different internal or external environment (our Beautifully Simple Model). This chapter looks at how change really happens, asking can people change and what is going on inside? In organizations change is often associated with some new learning, so we also look at how we can facilitate this happening most easily.

As Synaptic Potential works with a variety of different types of organizations, we have the privilege of observing some of the trends that come and go and how people really engage with what is being suggested. We approach things from a different perspective, the neuroscience perspective, but as we always maintain there are definite valuable links to other lenses. When we view things through different disciplines we see similarities and certainly practical applications. I'll always remember a team meeting at Bangor University where there was a neuroscientist, a psychologist, and a behavioral scientist all talking about the same project and concept. Each of them had a different term and slightly different understanding of it. They were all looking through different lenses and with different language and experiments to explain it. The great thing about bringing these all together is that we can gain a deeper appreciation of reality. Often with the addition of neuroscience we can add nuances from what we know about the brain to help organizations ensure they are getting the most out of tools and models that originate from other disciplines.

Neuroplasticity

Wherever I speak now, I ask people to put their hands up if they are familiar with neuroplasticity. Groups tend to be polarized in their responses: either they all have, or hardly anyone has – it is fascinating. My follow-up question to groups where most people have raised their hand is to ask who would like to give a short explanation. Normally the hands quickly disappear. There has been a lot of mixed writing around the topic of neuroplasticity. So let's clear a few things up.

Neuroplasticity is an umbrella term that encompasses various ways that the brain is plastic (or able to be changed) in nature. Where previously it was commonplace to believe that the brain in adulthood was relatively static and unchanging, now we understand that changes occur in the

neural pathways and synapses of the brain.[1] These changes occur naturally and as a result of changes in behavior, environment, thinking, and
emotion.[2]

There are a lot of reputable studies now published that share insights into
the plastic nature of the brain. Using functional magnetic resonance imaging (fMRI) we can see structural changes that occur in gray and white matter with learning. There is discussion around the cellular and molecular-level
changes that would account for the observable effects in imaging.[3] Over
the years some studies have become rather fashionable, even making it into
dinner party discussions with non-neuroscientists. Here are our top three:

1. *The Black Cab driver's hippocampus.*[4] This study found that the
   famous London Black Cab drivers had larger posterior hippocampal
   volumes than other people. You may be thinking, "That makes complete sense, since the hippocampus is involved in special navigation
   it follows that people who have such detailed knowledge of London
   roads and how to navigate them would have larger parts of the brain
   dedicated to doing that." Initially further questions were raised as to
   whether people who had this increased volume were attracted to the
   role, or whether actually doing the job changed the brain. Further
   studies have confirmed that the training increases the capacity.
2. *Juggling and the visual motion area.*[5] A longitudinal MRI study used
   voxel-based morphometry to show an increase in gray matter density
   in the visual motion area bilaterally when people learnt to juggle over
   three months. In a subsequent study changes were noted in the brain
   in as little as seven days.[6]
3. *Meditation and multiple brain changes.*[7] It has been found that training in meditation can induce changes in both specific brain networks
   and also changes in brain states. The efficiency of white matter has
   been shown to increase after even just a few hours of training. Some
   research suggests that the way meditation can work is by producing a
   molecular cascade that increases myelin and improves connectivity.

The first two changes fall under a researcher called Tang's classification
system of network training and the third type of changes are a result of

state training.[8] Network training normally involves the training of specific networks involved in processes such as motor activities (juggling) or working memory. State training relates to the states that occur in meditation or aerobic exercise.

We will come back to the benefits of meditation at a later point, for now it is well worth noting the plentiful research that shows that our brains can literally change and we benefit as a result of meditative practices.[9, 10, 11] Extrapolating from this, it would be fair to suggest that we give consideration to the bigger picture. Thinking only about 9am–5pm or, more realistically for many, 8am–7pm is nonsense.

our brains can literally change and we benefit as a result

The reality is that brain is being shaped all the time. So it is far from the case that mindfulness meditation is magic. (Unless you also consider everything else we do, from playing golf, cooking dinner, walking the dog, playing with a child, and so on, to be magic too). This gets us thinking, are you clear on the qualities you *really* want from your team members? How are you communicating that to them? Often in the organizations we work with we will hear people with senior, director, or manager in their title say that they are looking for one thing from people, for example honesty. However, they will not be being transparent when there are challenges, preferring to cover things up, and at times forcing people to lie or at best reveal that there are things that cannot be spoken about. This "do as I say, not as I do" approach is fundamentally flawed and creates many problems. Humans are wonderful modelers.

Another inconsistency we frequently see is around wellbeing and sleep. Organizations often say that they want highly productive, efficient, and effective employees; that their employees' wellbeing is important to them. They understand that for their staff to consistently perform at the top level (in fact at any level) it is important for them to be looked after. Ask them what the culture is around getting adequate sleep and you often see an area for improvement jumping out at you. Unless you and your colleagues are all regularly investing in getting good quality and quantity of sleep then meticulously pay attention to the suggestions made for change. It could dramatically transform your organization. We will look at this in more depth later in this chapter. At this point we are picking up some challenges organizations experience. It can be painful to take an honest look at things. Sometimes cultures encourage us to only focus on the positives, or at least not to talk about the negatives outside of an in-house meeting. However you do it, being able to honestly look at the reality is an important starting point.

How do we enhance the wiring in our brains?[12] Our environment offers us huge potential. It has long been known that the environment of animals has an impact on their brains.[13] In a specific study with rats, it was found that an exercise wheel, larger social groups, daily repositioning of food hoppers and various objects, and weekly cage changing heightened the brain plasticity.[14] Experiments with humans in real-life situations, that is, at work, are not yet mainstream. The potential to reshape organizations based on a reliable evidence base is exciting and perhaps a little overwhelming. We already know that engaging neuromodulatory systems such as acetylcholine and dopamine enhance sensory processing and brain plasticity.[15] We know the reward system uses dopamine, and action games that demand divided attention with efficient re-allocation as the tasks change probably engage these systems. However, translating this and other insights into the workplace is relatively uncharted.

We shall dive deeper into this in Chapter 5. At this point, we want to be aware that our environment is one of the shapers of our brain. Once leaders of organizations truly understand this they have big choices to make. Many environments people exist in are leading to unhappiness, lack of engagement, and lowered drive. Putting in place employee engagement initiatives, more rewards, or other surface-level ideas will only do so much. It can be scary to change the very fabric and organization of a company, but it may deliver the best results.

our environment is one of the shapers of our brain

A bridge between neuroplasticity and a psychological observation is the concept of a growth mindset. Carol Dweck, a psychology professor, has long shared her thoughts and research around the effects that a fixed mindset versus a growth mindset can have upon people. One longitudinal study examined the effect students' fixed mindset had, which was a downward academic trend. On the other hand, the math students with a growth mindset experienced progression. In another study, students were split into two groups, one were taught study skills and how they could learn to be smart (using the analogy of the brain as a muscle that could be strengthened the more it was used.) The other group were only taught study skills. In just two months the first group were outperforming the other group.[16]

Does your organization encourage, at all levels, in all ways, a growth mindset?

Memory

Understanding how our memory works is important when we think about change and especially when we consider learning. When we are learning things at work, most of the time we talk about trying to get things into our declarative (or explicit) memory. This concerns things that can be consciously recalled, such as facts and knowledge. The other type of long-term memory is procedural (or non-declarative) memory and this concerns unconscious memories such as skills, for example learning to ride a bicycle. There are two categories of declarative memory: semantic and episodic; we believe the latter provides support for the former. Semantic memories store general factual knowledge whereas episodic memories store chunks of observation information attached to a specific event. The more scientists learn about memory, the more they realize there is to learn! The entire brain is considered involved in memory, so it isn't that one area stores all the memories in filing cabinets.

How is all this relevant to learning? Well it is the mechanisms through which we get things into our brain. Some of the keys include:

- First, we need to pay attention to the thing we want to remember. So whether that is through being clear on the relevance, the personal

significance, it having an emotional draw, there being no other distractions, and so on, we have to initially pay attention to it.
• Then it needs to get into our working memory – we need to process it.
• Finally, with the involvement of the hippocampus, the memory is stored.

A three-stage model was developed by Eichenbaum and colleagues to suggest how the hippocampus works with episodic memory:

1. It mediates the recording of the episodic memory.
2. It identifies the common features between episodes.
3. It links these common episodes in a memory space (it networks them).

Linking things up, or networking things, is key to being able to recall things easily in the future. By repeatedly exposing ourselves to episodes we strengthen the links in the memory space, which makes it quicker for us to retrieve the information.[17] We also know that the activation in the hippocampus during the encoding process is related to a person's ability to recall the information.[18, 19, 20, 21]

Learning

Learning is a hugely important part of many organizations. The ability of the workforce to receive new information, digest it, and then think or behave differently as a result could be as vital as making or breaking a company. In today's rapidly changing times the need for people to be able to keep up is a real business case.

The learning and development "department" (learning and development are happening throughout the organization, aren't they?) may already have its own reputation and brand, which may be helping or hindering it. The overall strategies shared in Chapters 1 and 2 (results – behavior – environment and engage – motivate – manage) hold true for any learning and development. What we will focus on in this chapter is an additional body of research brought together into a checklist that will help you evaluate any L&D strategies from a neuroscience perspective.

Ultimately all learning happens inside an individual's brain. We cannot force someone to create new neural pathways, strengthen them, and reactivate them to recall the information or behaviors effectively. However, we can create an external environment (a learning environment and culture) that makes it easier.

When we work with organizations to create a strong learning culture we are looking at everything, like detectives. So we encourage you to do the same. Here we will focus in on one approach that takes you out of your day-to-day role. We need you to imagine you and any colleagues you select to join you in this exploration are each climbing into cranes and travelling way up high above your organization, so you've got a brilliant bird's-eye view of it. From your cranes you look down and assess how learning is happening at your place of work. You may choose to use the CRANES checklist on one particular learning initiative, the way a particular department learns, or learning overall. Before you get to **exploring** where you're at, let's look at what each of the components can **inform** us about.

Connection

Retrieval

Attention

Networks

Emotion

Sleep

It is also worth remembering these bits, which are nothing NEW. They are basics that are often forgotten by individuals.

Nutrition

Exercise

Water

> **GRAHAM SALISBURY – HEAD OF HR, ACTIONAID UK**
>
> I believe that learning takes place away from the lecture room. Therefore what we try to do is we try to create a culture where there are lots of different learning activities going on, so there are things such as learning circles. If there is an external expert who is able to talk about an issue – it might be tax avoidance, it could be human rights – we will form a learning circle to ask questions and those kind of things. We do quite a few informal "lunch and learn" kind of sessions, where we get people with an issue or with interest to get together and to talk about things like that.

Connection

We are social creatures. Social exclusion, a social pain, can bear a lot of resemblance to a physical pain.[22] Similarly, social pleasures, such as recognition, activate the brain's reward circuitry in a powerful way.[23] If we want people to be self-motivated and engaged in any learning process then we need it to be (at least) neurally pleasurable. We explore this in depth in Chapter 6.

Facilitating Connection

There are several things you can do to help facilitate connection. The first is to be aware of its importance. Be creative and flexible. Then consider:

- Face-to-face learning teams – interdepartmental groups that meet up to share what they are learning, share how they are applying it, and share their goals.
- Creating informal opportunities for learning – coffee and fruit salad sessions, walking debriefs, or simply chatting over lunch.
- Inviting people to share their stories of learning through writing, video, audio, or live presentations. (Stories, as we'll discover later, are very powerful.)

- Ensuring people feel comfortable and equipped to connect with their colleagues on how their learning is going.
- Mentoring, coaching and secondments.
- Buddy systems.
- Recognition – rather than a staged, tick-box approach to this, consider it a natural consequence when real connection forms between people and they genuinely care about their colleagues' learning experience and outcomes.

What This Doesn't Mean

This does not mean that everything needs to be done with other people. Some strategies may not need a specific "connection" piece.

Retrieval

The normal aim of learning is to be able to retrieve the information at some point. It is a little counter-intuitive that students often spend so much time trying to get the information in, but comparatively little time practicing getting it back out again. How activated the hippocampus is during the encoding process correlates with the ability to retrieve information.[18]

Facilitation of Retrieval

- Consider training people in strategies to retrieve the information that they are digesting.
- Build retrieval into any program designs.
- In our live training programs we play specially designed retrieval games that develop as the program progresses to enhance focus and expertise in retrieving information.
- For skills-based chunks invite people to practice things.
- Agree retrieval-based accountability once the initial learning period is finished (be that a training or on the job learning, and so on).

Cross-pollination Opportunity

Combine connecting people and retrieval:

- Encourage buddying up to process and consider applications of the learning.
- Create relaxed environments where people can share what they're learning and doing.

Note: Some organizations already have good programs and even retrieval practices in place, the opportunity there is to ensure the strategy overall is cohesive. Often we hear L&D teams working with a provider and simply adding more workshops during a year that don't actually fit into an overall solid strategy. This needs to be driven by the business objectives and deliver for the organization. With the move to more highly valuing the social learning there are normally opportunities to better embed the retrieval processes associated with that.

People are natural retrievers. However, many organizations have people so over stretched the idea of them daydreaming and playing with ideas or investing time in exploring how they will apply the information they have digested is unusual. Subsequently you get a much poorer return on investment.

Attention

An area of neuroscience that is well researched is that of our attention system. This is of huge interest to any organization. A person's attention is one of their most valuable resources and where they give it is of significance.

A person's attention is one of their most valuable resources

Some basic things to be aware of include:

- The attention system is anatomically separate from data-processing systems.
- There is an attention network, rather than a single anatomical area.
- Different areas carry out different functions.

Subsystems of attention include:

- Orienting to sensory events
- Detecting signals for conscious processing
- Maintaining an alert state[24]

Generally of importance to any organization are the insights around attention and cognitive load. The ability to focus attention has been shown to improve under task conditions of high perceptual load. However, it decreases under conditions of high load on cognitive control processes. Working memory is a good example of these.[25]

Imagine a modern workplace today. You need to write a report. You've come into the office and your first task is to find a hot desk. You sit down and open your laptop. All around you are people busily typing away. Some are chatting. You haven't sat in this seat before and your eyes are drawn to the poster on the wall. Drawing your eyes back to your half-written piece you start to re-read what you last wrote. You find yourself reading the same bit over and over again while trying to block out the person talking on the telephone next to you. You are tapped on the shoulder, "I didn't realize you'd be in today, I just wanted to ask you about..." As you refocus on the paper you can't quite remember what you were thinking of when you wrote that last sentence. It is now deleted.

Shaping Attention

It appears that our attention skills can be conditioned. Research has shown that action video game play improves attentional resources.[26] This could be a matter for individual personal development. It doesn't often feature in KPIs, however the value to both the individual and the organization are high. Practicing mindfulness alone, being present with children, playing sport, playing musical instruments, and many other activities also could reasonably be expected to improve our ability pay attention.

Networks

Essentially when we learn something new we want to store it in our brains in a way that best positions it to be easily recalled when we need it. Imagine having lots of keywords or category labels attached to a blog post, or a business card filed under lots of different search terms, or storing a lip gloss in every bag – you want to be able to find what you are looking for easily. An idea or concept needs to hook into pre-existing ideas within our brain. Movie pitches are renowned for hooking into pre-existing networks – "*Speed* will be *Die Hard* on a bus" or "*Air Force One* will be *Die Hard* on a plane." *Die Hard* was a strong formula in the movie world and so many subsequent movies utilized that.

An idea or concept needs to hook into pre-existing ideas within our brain

Facilitating Networking

As you'll have realized by now this unfortunately doesn't mean scheduling lots of parties. There are still plenty of things you can do though:

- Ask people to sort through information and pull out the relevant pieces.
- Encourage people to create their own models or checklists or mnemonics.
- Suggest people share how they would explain what has just happened; this is great for retrieval as well as networking.
- Give people clear analogies, metaphors, and examples to hook the new information into.

Emotion

Experientially we have seen that emotion can be useful to the learning process. When we have an emotional response to something our attention is piqued and we get present and become engaged. The amygdala is an important part of the brain involved in processing emotions. Anatomically it is positioned next to the hippocampus and it is as though the amygdala gives the hippocampus a nudge to tell it to pay attention. Reward-motivated learning has importance here, too. Consider the state people are in just before learning something. Activating the reward networks precedes memory formation.[27]

Facilitating Emotion

- Consider adapting any experiences in current trainings that invoke negative emotions in people, for example, fear. Although it can be powerful, it can have negative side effects, such as decreased innovation.
- Create opportunities for people to be happy, to feel a sense of achievement, to acknowledge one another.
- Do things that are fun and that make people laugh.
- Be mindful of the state people are in before and during learning something.

Sleep

When was the last month you and your colleagues consistently got the amount of sleep you needed? Most people don't get as much sleep as they would like and feel they need. Insufficient sleep has been linked with less innovation,[28] lower job satisfaction,[29] and unethical behavior at work.[30]

Just to be clear (in case you haven't been getting your quota recently), the sleep crisis includes:

- Lack of sleep negatively affects productivity and innovation – the prefrontal cortex is affected and this can be from just 24 hours of sleep loss.

- Stress – sleep deprivation can raise stress hormone levels. Stress can impact sleep; an unfortunate cycle ensues.
- Sleeping with your smartphone – not switching off can have negative consequences.

Napping can help – consider 30 minutes maximum and between 2–3pm. What can you do about people's sleep? Potentially a lot. One could have asked a similar question about drinks at lunchtime or smoking at work and both of these behaviors are largely a thing of the past. Organizations have a lot of different approaches at their fingertips to help shape behaviors that benefit individuals and organizations.

1. Run a program that equips people with information on how to set themselves up for success. This includes sleep-awareness topics ranging from the importance of sleep to how to monitor your own sleep habits. It is easy to train people to filter down the information that could help people live a better quality of life. Better at home; better at work.
2. Re-design jobs so sleep deprivation is not a requirement. My friends at medical school were at the end of the crazy work hour's culture, however many still found themselves working 24-hour shifts. Would you want someone operating on you who had been awake for 17 hours? How about fighting a legal case for you? If we value what we do then it follows to want to do it to the best of our ability, and this then requires that we get adequate sleep.
3. Use technology to help not hinder. Most CEOs and senior leaders we have worked with have emails coming through to their mobile device 24 hours a day. In 2011, Volkswagen took the bold move to stop emails routing to employees when they are off shift. The default is now that people cannot access new emails. It certainly sends a bold message.
4. Create a culture that endorses sleep. Upon joining a new organization you are very susceptible to being influenced by the behaviors of the existing employees. Many organizations would like to think that they support people's "right" to get a good night's sleep. Unfortunately, too many still have cultures that encourage more of a workaholic

approach and a competitive vibe that is linked to getting just a few hours' sleep.

Nothing NEW

This section should be nothing new to most people. However, taking a snapshot in many organizations you probably wouldn't think that. There are many things you can do to help make change easier. The top three basic concepts are: Nutrition, Exercise, and Water. If people get good nutrition and hydration and add exercise into the mix then they are more likely to be able to change, to be "fit for change" as it were. You may think that as an organization you have nothing to do with a person's nutrition or exercise – well, our peers are important in shaping our behavior so we believe an organization can help influence even these basic behaviors. Alternatively you may be already embracing some ways to help people do the things we know are good for them and be looking to do more.

ANGELA O'CONNOR – DIRECTOR, HR LOUNGE

Some of the things that we know, we know instinctively or they are just part of our own collection, are the things that help make life doable and enjoyable. The basics like sleep, seven to eight hours a day. I have a really busy lifestyle: I run a business, I'm the president of the HR society, I'm a visiting professor, I've got a family, elderly parents, loads of things, but my day starts with 20 minutes' meditation followed by an hour's exercise, followed something decent to eat. Then I start work. Otherwise I couldn't do the things I do.

Nutrition

Fuel yourself well. We don't need to go into the details on this here. You know what good nutrition looks like. Ask yourself what the culture is like? Is there a 3pm chocolate round or are people inspired by others' seed collections?

Exercise

Today most people know that exercise is good for them. It has benefits for the body and mind. Just in case there was any doubt left, here are three studies that give us some additional insight into why every person in every organization should be exercising.

1. Exercise has been shown to influence brain plasticity and function by modulating brain-derived neurotrophic factor.[31]
2. Short bouts of mild-intensity exercise improve spatial learning and memory. Similarly to the previous study, hippocampal plasticity is involved.[32]
3. Aerobic exercise improves cognitive function in humans and rodents. A short period of high-intensity cycling resulted in enhancements in a face–name matching task. After five weeks of aerobic training increases in fitness, cognitive function, and serum BDNF response to acute exercise were seen.[33]

Exercise-induced cognitive enhancement is not recognized by many organizations. In the spirit of full disclosure we should note that a couple of these experiments were done with rats, however it is believed there are many similarities with humans, which the third paper illustrates. The evidence for exercising to equip our brain to be "change ready" is compelling.

With all the consideration now being given to the different generations that are valued contributors to the work force, we are sometimes asked what the research says about older people. Overall the evidence suggests that fitness training has robust benefits for executive control processes.[33] Cardiovascular fitness is thought to offset declines in cognitive performance. This is great news for any older workforces.[34]

The question could then be, if we all know that exercise is good for us, why aren't we all doing it? The answer often brings us back to the habits that we have in our organizations (closely linked to the culture) and our personal habits. What is possible? There are organizations out there where exercise is viewed as a normal behavior and it would be unusual for you not to have some sort of routine. In the UK this isn't yet the majority of organizations, as far as we have seen.

Consider these opportunities, and what you could do differently:

- How do you get to work?
- What do you do during meetings with others?
- How do you break up your day?
- What do you do at lunchtime?

Water

Drink it. Encourage others to do so too.

Next Steps

Once you have got these ticked off your checklist, the next stage is to work on the stickiness of your learning initiatives and how to package, market, and deliver things to get the next level of results. Once again, neuroscience can shed powerful light on how best to do this. Check out the book's website for details www.engagedbrains.com.

Tempted by Trends

Some L&D departments pride themselves on being aware of the latest trends. There is a question around whether chasing "what's hot" each year will deliver the best results. Through delivering our "Essential Neuroscience for L&D" program we have discovered, for example, that while many organizations are enthusiastic about the concept of 70:20:10, few know how to, in one company's word's "do it properly." It is an interesting response when we look at how the learning and development model came about. McCall, Lombardo, and Eichinger carried out a survey of high-performing managers that said:[35]

> Lessons learned by successful and effective managers are roughly:
> 70 percent from tough jobs
> 20 percent from people (mostly the boss)
> 10 percent from courses and reading

Piecing together bits doesn't shout strong and unified strategy. Investing in clarity and strong foundations helps you to pick and choose which white rabbits are worth following.

The outcome from the program we take teams through is three-fold, we recommend this approach. Firstly to **inform** L&D professionals about the latest neuroscience research that should be taken into consideration when creating and implementing any strategy. Secondly to **explore** what currently is happening. What are the current strengths of what you are doing, measured against a neuroscience-based criteria? Thirdly we want to **apply** what you've learnt to a specific project you are working on. One of the questions we ask up front is around how L&D is seen within the organization and what leverage the department has. The reason for this is that one of the biggest challenges is to link things up. Just like in the brain, something in isolation, without connections to everything else gets left out and eventually is weakened. So a big focus is about how we link things together. During the "apply" section we are scanning for opportunities within the bigger picture to tie things together and slot in neuroscience underpinned concepts to bring strategies to life and increase their effectiveness.

Neuroscience has a lot to offer the practical world of L&D, however it does this through grounded research and a thorough understanding of the brain. Then by understanding the context in which people and strategies are trying to work. Finally, by applying the information across the whole of the organization, not just in one department. Everything linking up is really crucial to getting the best results.

Here are some insights from an organization we worked with who are committed to 70:20:10 being far more than a passing trend.

LYANN FARRELLY – LEARNING & ORGANIZATIONAL DEVELOPMENT DIRECTOR, EUROPE, WARNER BROS

When implementing a strategy based on the principles of 70:20:10, for me, the learning culture of an organization has to be ready. 70:20:10 requires the whole business to think differently about L&D; this isn't just about getting them to consider learning solutions as more than training courses, this requires a culture of self-empowerment – for individuals and leaders to take ownership and to build their expertise in having good development conversations. To take this even a step further, the L&D team (not solely their responsibility but realistically where this will start) have a responsibility to ignite an excitement and energy about learning.

Many learners in corporate organizations, although [they] enjoy the experience of going on a training course, don't always actively seek learning opportunities and are passive, waiting for a performance review or waiting for their managers to suggest solutions. This puts a great deal of pressure on managers and managers don't feel confident in their knowledge and expertise to identify learning opportunities outside of a list of scheduled training courses that they themselves have experienced or recognize.

The 70 Percent

As an L&D function we need to work with individuals on helping them see their own role and take responsibility for their own development. We also need to work with leaders (and individuals) to help them understand the principles of 70:20:10, which, by the way, most leaders completely subscribe to often being cited as a "no brainer." We then need to equip the leader with the information they need to have great development conversations: building their capabilities around curiosity, listening, and questioning but also their confidence. When working with leaders they often have great ideas around the 70 percent and let's face it they are the best placed to identify these opportunities, e.g. swapping team roles around, working on a project, and so on. The key thing here is that the learner is exposed to applying their learning in a real environment. There has to also be a degree of "it's safe to fail," which does make leaders nervous, they have to find their own level of comfort here.

The 20 Percent

I have had many leaders cite someone else in their team as having great capabilities in an area that another individual doesn't – when asking them the question – so why not peer mentor? Often they answer, that's a great idea and gives the other individual a new challenge and skill set. The 20 percent doesn't have to be a formal coaching and mentoring program. We run a reverse mentoring scheme where junior team members mentor our leaders. We also run lunch-and-learns where people in the business share their knowledge with others – this blurs the lines of 70:20:10 but it doesn't really matter as they are hugely successful for many reasons.

The 10 Percent

We need to recognize the process of embedding learning and that a learner has experienced all of the input, guidance, and ongoing experience that a good 70:20:10 solution should provide. For example, all training solutions should reference the 70 and 20 percent solutions which would support the learning, design should include experiential learning techniques such as role plays and business simulations, use peer mentoring, and action learning groups – not just relying on the course facilitator – and bringing real business issues to training courses are also great ways to leverage the 70 percent and 20 percent. I think my point here is that we shouldn't be purest about this, clearly offering separate solutions within the 70:20:10, we can blur the lines.

Designing business, team, and individual training plans with leaders to include the 70 and 20 as well as the 10 is key. Allowing easy access to solutions which may include investment in technology/mobile learning to support self-directed learning, budgeting appropriately, and ensuring processes support the concept, e.g., that managers have pre- and post-course conversations: pre-, what is your objective? how will you implement this in the work environment?; post-, did you achieve your objective? have you and will you continue to implement this in the work environment? Rather than the traditional "seeking approval" process.

In summary, I believe it's really about educating and empowering the business to take their learning seriously, to approach it in a way that intuitively and scientifically we know works and to take responsibility – leaders and managers in particular – they are at the coal face of the 70 percent and key to this strategy working in partnership with their L&D teams.

When Is the Time Right?

Now you know the science behind how change really happens. That isn't the end of the story though. Many organizations will be aware of some of the key concepts that are explained as we move forward, however they will not have acted on them. What are you waiting for? A disaster? A merger? Neil shared his thoughts just a year after going through a big merger.

NEIL MORRISON – HR DIRECTOR, RANDOM HOUSE GROUP

Too many organizations don't self-evaluate, don't stop to think. How many times I've said this next sentence, "But we have once-in-a-lifetime opportunity to reappraise our organization, because we have to look at every single piece, because we've got two organizations coming together." Not many organizations have the opportunity to do that unless they have something catastrophic happen to them. So in most organizations there is no momentum to look at what you do, to reappraise it, and change, because we've done alright so we will carry on doing alright. That has been built up over years of tweaks and changes and so you end up with something that is totally confusing for most employees. Most employees, I fundamentally believe, do not understand how their organizations work. They have absolutely no idea how stuff gets done, other than their bit. It's like a cubical culture without the cubical, it's quite incredible. A lot of that is because we've over-managed organizations and made them ridiculously complex. Why would you look at it if you've been successful after a period of time? [...] Why would you bother? Because you're kind of OK. We use the example of your health, so I know that I should probably drink a bit less, I should do a little more exercise, and I should have more fresh fruit and vegetables. I know this to be true yet there is nothing really wrong with me, I'm feeling OK....

It's only when you have a heart attack or something else happens to cause you to really reappraise that you often find the momentum to be able to really evaluate and lead to that behavior change, which is ultimately what we are asking organizations to do. [...]I think for leaders it's hard to change that unless.... So when does it happen? It often happens when a new CEO comes in and says, I want to do this; [it] very rarely happens when an HR director comes in, because the CEO will say, I want you to do this; or it happens when you go through a crisis like the BBC, for example, where you've got to go in and look all over it again. So in many ways I'm not surprised because, why would you?

What's the Bottom Line?

Neuroplasticity means change is possible.

Learning should be, at least neurally, rewarding.

What Can I Do Today?

Invest in Quality Sleep

Take responsibility for your own revitalizing sleep. Each night practice good "sleep hygiene," which is the practice of controlling "all behavioural and environmental factors that precede sleep and may interfere with sleep."[36] According to the National Sleep Foundation, good sleep hygiene includes things like:[37]

- Avoiding stimulants such as caffeine, nicotine, and alcohol close to bedtime. Alcohol may help you get to sleep quicker but can disrupt your sleep in the second half of the night as you metabolize it.
- Get enough exercise. Specifically, do vigorous exercise in the morning or late afternoon and save yoga for before bed to help get you ready for a peaceful night.
- Have your largest meal earlier in the day and if you are partial to a little chocolate have that earlier too (remembering it contains caffeine).
- Get plenty of natural light – it helps maintain your sleep–wake cycle.
- Establish and defend a relaxing bedtime routine – avoid negative thoughts and ruminating.
- Keep your bed for sleep (as opposed to watching television).

What Can I Put in Place for the Long Term?

- Create an opportunity to discuss CRANES with your team.
- The next stages may involve running programs that upskill people in alignment with the strategy.
- Explore starting exercise classes during lunch breaks on site.

What Is the Overall Ideal Vision?

People Getting into CRANES

On a regular basis L&D teams, and possibly others, taking time out to get a bird's-eye view of what is happening within the organization and make strategic tweaks.

Healthy Sleep Attitude

The vision is for the culture of the organization to support and encourage healthy sleep attitudes and practices. Gone will be the days where people compete to be the last one leaving the office, downing the most caffeine the next morning, or looking the most wiped out.

Positivity towards Nutrition, Exercise, and Water

Our peers have a big influence on us. Imagine an organization filled with people who all exercised at some point during their day. People could live longer, more healthily, more happily, and be more productive.

part II

How Do We Engage People?

Key Takeaways

- What engagement actually is.
- How to engage a brain.
- The concept you have to build everything else around.

How Do We Engage Our Employees?

The question of how to engage our employees is a big one. Engagement is a term that has been in circulation for a long time, undergoing trendy times and times of less favor. Historically the approach has been to observe people. Now we have the opportunity to look through the deeper lens of neuroscience to see what goes on in the brain and add this to what has been known before.

We are wired to engage in a variety of different ways. Getting clear on what would result when someone is engaged may be a good first step. Essentially our brain can be engaged when a range of different things are going on internally and externally. Looking outside of the world of business we can sometimes take back valuable insights. Consider a child for a moment, playing with her favorite toy, making up stories about the adventures it has been on – would you say she was engaged? How about a teenager heading out on with his skateboard for the fourth time that day to practice his 360 flip? A couple at dinner looking longingly into each other's eyes on their first anniversary? The volunteers at their local soup kitchen on their days off doing the cleaning up after serving lunch to homeless people? The list could go on.

What Is Engagement?

We're thinking about "what is an engaged brain?" Getting into the world of semantics, which we often do when trying to bridge insights from neuroscience to the language organizations can relate to, we can struggle with exact translations. There are many definitions of engagement out there along with a question around whether engagement is an attitude, a behavior, or an outcome. I'm not going to propose an answer to that question, but offer instead another perspective.

If we look back at:

- The child playing with her toy
- The teenager practicing his skateboard tricks
- The couple connecting deeply
- The volunteer giving their time and energy

and consider whether they could be considered to be engaged, then it points us to areas of neuroscience research previously not linked to engagement. Qualities of engagement normally include:

- A heightened emotional connection
- An influence to exert greater discretionary effort[1]
- Commitment
- Willingness to help out
- Something that is offered, cannot be required[2]

This part of the book explores the research and practical applications that stem from a different perspective on engagement. It would still be expected, even with the various routes to engagement, that many of the benefits would be the same:

- Happier
- Healthier
- More fulfilled
- Focused
- Advocates of the organization
- More productive
- Take more sleep and exercise
- Good cognitive functioning
- Meeting people out of work

Neuroscience shares with us what is going on in the brain when we can expect to see these benefits and more. Our focus, then, is how to create these situations in the brain.

What Might You Already Be Doing?

Engage For Success, a movement committed to "the idea that there is a better way to work, a better way to enable personal growth, organisational growth and ultimately growth for Britain by releasing more of the capability and potential of people at work," suggests that there are four enablers of engagement useful to organizations to evaluate the effectiveness of their approaches.

1. Visible, empowering leadership providing a **strong strategic narrative** about the organization, where it's come from, and where it's going.
2. **Engaging managers** who focus their people and give them scope, treat their people as individuals, and coach and stretch their people.
3. There is **employee voice** throughout the organizations, for reinforcing and challenging views, between functions and externally; employees are seen as central to the solution.

4. There is organizational **integrity** – the values on the wall are reflected in day-to-day behaviors. There is no "say–do" gap.

Existing approaches give some people an opportunity to try to reverse engineer how they might work. The other approach is to go direct to the neuroscience.

What Most Organizations Are Not Yet Sculpting Their Approach Around

At Synaptic Potential we hold a big toolkit of research and applications drawn from this, which we use when we team up with organizations to make a change. Throughout this part of the book we zoom into several networks of great importance to the various ways engagement can be created and the effects it can have. The first is the reward network and is one of the primary ways an individual can create desirable results. There are lots of ways to activate this network, in Chapter 3 we focus on a big one that we suggest you build everything else around. In subsequent chapters we build-in additional valuable concepts you should be aware of. The opportunity is to consider some key insights taken from neuroscience research that can positively shape your organization to become more successful, both for those you serve and those who are doing the serving.

Reward Networks

Why do we want people activating their reward networks?

- They experience an increase in cognitive resources.[3]
- They are more creative.[4]
- They can solve more problems, using insight (especially useful for complex problem solving).[5]
- They come up with more action-focused ideas.[6]
- They have a broader field of view.[7]

You'll notice the similarities in the themes between what happens when people's reward networks are activated and the benefits we expect to see from engaged employees. The striatum releases dopamine into the prefrontal cortex and anterior cingulate cortex, which positively affects a range of cognitive and emotional functions. When individuals have good levels of dopamine in the executive attention or self-regulation networks, we should see the attitude, behavior, and outcomes of engagement.

A Word of Warning

With so much available on such an, at times, hot topic, it pays to be cautious. If you've come across an exercise to do with your team that promises "increased engagement," pause to consider how it might work. Sometimes doing ad hoc pieces can damage an organization's culture rather than enhance it. There is rarely a substitute for a well-planned, well-executed strategy.

The Concept You Have to Build Everything Else Around

chapter 4

Key Takeaways

- It activates the reward network – it makes us feel good and makes us want to do it again.
- It connects us – to what we're doing, why we're doing it, and what effect it has (great to have that feedback loop).
- We can help people identify the contribution they are already making.

Solid Engagement

This chapter is about laying the foundations for really solid engagement. There are potential pitfalls along the journey. However, the neural and experiential rewards are considerable if you can master this. Consider some of the times you have recently felt deeply engaged. Think about experiences that you can really remember well. Classic examples that often stand out for people have the quality of helping others in some way. Within us is programming that makes helping others make us feel good. Maybe you got together with a group of other people when someone asked you for help. Running a 5k to raise money for charity, organizing a fundraising event, or staying on with your team to work on a project for a client late into the evening. Instances when you are clear on the contribution you are making tend to grab us and form solid memories. Often there are less clear links to how we are helping. Perhaps working on a report or giving a presentation or even tidying up the messy kitchen hasn't been giving you that same feeling.

Remember the story of President Kennedy's visit to the NASA space center in 1962? He noticed a janitor carrying a broom and walked over to the man saying, "Hi, I'm Jack Kennedy. What are you doing?" The janitor responded, "I'm helping put a man on the moon, Mr President."

For employees to have that level of connection with the contribution that they are making is a wonderful thing. We can imagine that the janitor:

• Took pride in his work, doing it to the best of his abilities
• Was excited to go to work on Mondays and felt fulfilled on Fridays
• Would speak positively about his organization.

Contribution

In Jim Collins's wonderful book *Built to Last* we hear about the research that compares 18 pairs of companies.[1] They had an average age of 100 years and had stock performing 15 times better than the overall stock market. Each visionary company was paired with a comparison company. One of their findings was that the visionary companies were guided more by a core ideology. They had values and a purpose beyond making money. In our language, they were clear on what they were contributing. Collins shares that they chose the word *ideology* because they observed what was an almost religious fervor in these companies. The core ideology was pursued zealously and was preserved to guide future generations.

Parallels can be drawn with the influential Theodore Roosevelt Malloch's thinking; he said, a "visionary company understands profit in the way that the biologist understands oxygen – not the goal of life, but the thing without which there is no life."[2] Simon Sinek has gathered a large following through sharing this message.[3] He suggests that all organizations know what they do. Many know how they do it. He says very few know why they do it. He suggests that knowing your why, your purpose, your cause, your belief, is important. Asking why you get out of bed in the morning, why anyone should care are important questions. Since my first book, *Make Your Brain Work*, was published, we have been asking the organizations we work with in workshops why their organization deserves to exist: an emotive and charged question that normally stumps people initially.

Organizations are understandably interested in what the bottom line return is when learning about new things and investing resources in developing the business. By getting clear on what contribution is being made the expected result down the line is a healthier company – borne out as far as stock prices. However, the irony is that isn't the driver for the companies that are already clear. More research would need to be done to see how the process evolved and whether any negatively influencing factors interfered.

The research from Collins, along with a lot of other research, is not new. It has been available for organizations to learn from for many years. Why then does it not *really* underpin how most organizations work? We have one of those wonderful times when neuroscience offers a deeper insight into what could be going on here. It doesn't replace some of the excellent research that has been done through other disciplines previously. Nor does it disprove what thoughtful thinkers have come up with before. In this case, it simply offers an additional perspective.

Neuroscience of Contribution

With a lack of neuroscience evidence gathered from the workplace setting, we turn to other hard neuroscientific research. In this case, looking at charitable donation, that is, contributing to a cause. In this experiment, the participants chose to endorse or oppose societal causes by anonymous decisions to donate or refrain from donating to real charitable organizations.[4] These organizations had a range of different causes. The mesolimbic reward system (ventral tegmental area – striatum) is engaged when people contribute to charities in the same way as when they receive monetary rewards. This reward system provides a general reinforcement mechanism. Interestingly in this study they also saw medial orbitofrontal-subgenual and lateral orbitofrontal areas (involved in primitive mechanisms of social attachment and aversion) involved in the decisions of whether to donate or oppose societal causes. It was also seen that more anterior sectors of the prefrontal cortex were recruited when altruistic choices were made above selfish material ones. It is suggested that primitive reward and social attachment operate beyond our immediate kin, enabling us to directly link motivational value to abstract collective causes, principles and ideologies.[5]

A groundbreaking experiment demonstrated that social values emerge from coactivation of stable abstract social conceptual representations in the superior anterior temporal lobe and context-dependent moral sentiments encoded in fronto-mesolimbic regions.[5] People can feel pride and gratitude in relation to their work, this will activate the mesolimbic and basal forebrain.

What Do We Need to Know About Contributing?

- People asked to commit five acts of kindness on one day a week for six weeks were happier than those who didn't do this.[6]
- The emotional benefits of helping others are eliminated when you are told you "should" help – so autonomy and personal volition are key.[7]
- Successfully completing actions is important (setting goals that can be finished).[8]
- Empathy, linked to the release of oxytocin, promotes prosocial behaviors such as collective action.[9]

In another experiment the researchers looked at when *giving* leads to happiness. The first study drew upon previous evidence that giving feels good. Using our time and money to benefit other people often delivers emotional rewards for the giver. They looked at contributing to two different causes and the one that came out tops was the one that more clearly identified how the contribution would help recipients. Participants contributed more and experienced higher happiness afterwards. At this point they couldn't prove that the difference in prosocial impact caused differences in the emotional benefits so another study was set up. This study provided more support to the idea that prosocial impact moderates the emotional benefits of prosocial spending.[10]

Altruism at Work?

Are there any parallels between giving to a charity and being paid to work in an organization? Possibly. It is conceivable that once the financial remuneration box has been checked adequately, then attention and drive in the brain is conditioned and focused by things other than money. Approaching it from the other angle, initially we make a decision as to which organization we will give our time to. Time is one of our most precious commodities. Many things are often considered. We may think that once that decision is made we don't have to give our choice much more thought. In reality we are making decisions every day. Many of our daily behaviors are shaped by our habits, but our habits are still being shaped by what goes on around us. If a person is becoming less engaged with their organization you will tend to notice them becoming more engaged with other things, searching for ways to activate their reward networks. Maybe it is social media during work time, perhaps gossip, eating more chocolate, or even daydreaming. Our brains seek out reward.

Organizations ask for time, energy, commitment, focus, loyalty, your presence, self-improvement, drive, and many of these qualities or states that link to desirable behaviors are also linked to the reward network in the brain.

In return they can offer many things to individuals. Ultimately organizations *could* offer people the awareness that they are doing something valuable with their 9am–5pm time investment daily. Instead of the American Red Cross's advertisement "Feel good about yourself – Give blood!" imagine the effect of "Feel good about yourself – work here!" In order for this to be easiest though it would help if leaders could articulate the value the organization offers.

Applications at Work

The opportunity here is to align everything. Too often in organizations things are disparate and this dramatically reduces the effectiveness of everything. The entrepreneurially spirited organizations or ones that have managed to retain their contribution concept as they grow (presuming it was there and strong to start with) have a distinct advantage. However, if you find your organization identifying this as an area for growth, then you can tackle it one piece at a time. Your life will be easier if you dedicate some time to getting clear on the strategy first. Invest time in getting clear before you start implementing anything.

When I interviewed Amy from EY, I noticed a real strength in her approach. She placed strategy first and then sought out opportunities to link things up. Essentially it was like she was networking all of her messages together, anchoring them into different opportunistic places within the business. Just like the brain's ability to recall, that we saw in Chapter 3, I'm sure this has helped engagement with one of her projects grow from six people to 250 within a year. Some people might dismiss things happening in a big firm as too different a context to theirs, or believe that they have lots of resources to throw at projects. However, Amy is an entrepreneur and used to boot-strapping to get things done. The strength here is in the approach, which can be borrowed and utilized in any sized organization.

Amy also credits her colleagues with the success of the approach.

> One of the things I've been so lucky with here, and one of the reasons it has worked is that from day one is that Paul Quinlan, our lead in

Employee Relations has been more than supportive of me. Paul, myself, and Susie Gray (also from Employee Relations) basically developed everything and brought it all together. We've also had amazing support from the UK HR director and other people, including a very senior sponsor Steve Wilkinson, our UK Head of Markets. We have achieved a lot, got a lot more to do, and it's because people have bought into it and haven't seen it as a threat. People have let us do what we wanted to do.

AMY MCKEOWN – HEALTH, MENTAL HEALTH, AND WELL-BEING, EY

Health EY was launched in February 2014, having been in planning since July 2013. It is the firm's approach to health, mental health, and well-being. We believe that physical health and mental health are as important as each other and we also focus as much on prevention as we do cure. Underpinning all of what we do is solid KPI and ROI analysis.

Human beings are animals not machines. However, we work in an accountancy firm and we're always talking about being efficient and productive. So instead when we talk about health we use organic language. Trees have roots and branches. We talk about flourishing, nurturing, thriving. Things you wouldn't expect to see in our firm. Underneath Health EY are six roots. These roots are shared on a postcard, which all new joiners get and we hand out freely.

Root 1: The nature of being human is having needs that reflect this, respect your body / mind and learn to work with them not against them.

Root 2: Your emotional health is as important as your physical health.

Root 3: It is your responsibility to look after your health and mental health and to ensure the people working with you are doing the same. Health EY will provide the power and tools to do that. (We try to treat our workforce as a professional, capable workforce. We are not talking about five-a-day here.)

**Root 4: Being healthy is all about making small, positive
changes in everyday life.** (So we're not trying to get a load
of competitive athletes to do an ironman. It's about drinking
water, walking, engaging everybody not just the super fit.)

**Root 5: The nature of being human is having times of ill
health such as cold, flu, anxiety or depression. These are
only instances and do not define you.** (This is crucial to me
because as a firm, no one remembers if you get the flu, but if
you have anxiety against you … It will take five years before
this seeps into our DNA but it is clearly there.)

**Root 6: Good health is both a personal asset and a business
asset.** (So this underpins everything we do.)

These are the roots to my programme.

Health EY also has nurture and thrive. Thrive is prevention.
Nurture is the cure when you're sick. Under the banner of
thrive we have a quarterly programme of events interchanging
quarters on physical and mental health. It includes topics such
as sleep, eating healthily, cognitive skills and resilience. We
have two to three webinars a month. Our health provider and
occupational health team help to run these. It is important to us
that it isn't just me talking about sleep, it is someone who works
in a Harley street sleep clinic talking about sleep. Our food and
mood theme is addressed by a nutritionalist and a psychologist.
We also have office-based events. Generally Nuffield, who are
our health care provider, run events on the quarterly theme in
every main office in the UK and the webinars are run by Rood
Lane, our occupational health provider.

We choose the topics based on our health screening stats. We
work on the principle of educate, educate, educate. Some other
topics include body clocks and circadian rhythms, the psychological aspect of performance, posture (specifically spinal
health), and managing mood (from positive mood through to
depression). Some people won't know about Health EY for two

to three years but it's about organic growth and over time creating a healthier workforce.

We try to link things together. For example, our posture section involves working with a musculoskeletal team, physiologists, physiotherapists but also it is a time to talk about work place assessments and things like that. When we do healthy eating we have all of the cafes involved. Our intention is to link everything together. So people going for health assessments get told what is happening each quarter.

Where Should You Network Contribution?

The aim is for any message to be consistent throughout the entire organization. We want to hook into anywhere it makes sense. For most organizations this means some changes need to happen. It also means you'll need to engage various people in what contribution they'll be making by helping you do this. Here is a non-exhaustive list of places, processes, and general tools to consider reviewing for consistency of message:

- Strategy
- Public and in-house events
- Sales and marketing
- Customer relations
- Employee relations
- Product or service development and delivery
- Accounting
- Training and development
- Decision making
- Recruitment process
- Induction process
- Pay and reward
- Language used
- Visuals around the workplace

There are so many ways of bringing to the forefront people's contribution at work. To be clear, the ideal is to draw it out of their daily job. In addition to that, there are other ways to enrich people's working life and help others at the same time. We find robust evidence that volunteers are more satisfied with their life than non-volunteers.[11] This is something that many organizations utilize in a way that everyone benefits from. At EY they have various networks, for example EY Black Network, EY Disability Working Group, EY Interfaith Working Group. Volunteers run all these groups.[12]

AMY MCKEOWN – HEALTH, MENTAL HEALTH AND WELL-BEING, EY

The mental health network one of our Disability Working Groups. I took over it in January 2013 when there were just four members. After I'd looked at what the firm was doing for six months I started a monthly network call. I started to think about what we as a network could offer to the rest of the firm.

We now run speaker events two to three times a year. We have a range of different speakers, from Oliver James, the author of *Affluenza*, who was talking about the psychological aspect of performance to the journalist Justin Hardy, and even Steve Peters, author of *The Chimp Paradox*. Our aim is to reduce the stigma. We want people to come and talk about mental health as being a normal aspect of health without it being, "Oh my gosh, I've had depression" type thing. We average around 150 people at these events.

The second thing the network offers is support. Quite a few people, when I started doing work in mental health, came to share with me their experience with the firm, whether good or bad. People said to me that when they returned from having depression they could have really done with having someone to talk to who had been off with depression. We started promoting a buddy network. The premise of it is that we have 12,500 employees in the UK, a large population where someone somewhere, has probably experienced the same thing as you whatever that is. It's just a question of finding them so that you can support or be supported by someone who has been through a similar experience. So we have all our formal HR processes but this is an informal network where we'll pair you up, you arrange a cup of tea and a chat. It is not designed to be a counselling session, and in fact we put some quite strict criteria around it. We use the coaching relationship boundary standards and things like that. As it stands we have 80 buddies, more on the list, and we have 30 buddy relationships. It is a very nice thing to have, informal and confidential.

The network has now grown to 250 people and we have a region rep in almost every office in the UK (20 out of 22). Last week was Time to Talk day, so there was something going on all over the place – a Samaritan came to talk in Birmingham there was a Time to Talk breakfast in Glasgow. The network is now our biggest disability network at the firm. Once we got people talking about it, it just grew and grew.

The Value of Emotion

Joseph LeDoux wrote in his wonderful book *The Emotional Brain* that he first started working on the brain mechanisms of emotion in the late 1970s when very few scientists were interested in the topic. Sometimes it feels like some organizations are just catching up. LeDoux views emotions as "biological functions of the nervous system" and suggests that by "figuring out how emotions are represented in the brain can help us understand them." He points out, even back in 1999, that this approach is different from the psychological approach of seeing emotions as states. It is worth sharing that coaches going through our Neuroscience for Coaches program often experience a big learning curve. They come in with questions primed by their non-neuroscience filters and experience. They ask things like "What is the neuroscience behind the primary emotions?" LeDoux says, "Psychological research has been extremely valuable, but an approach where emotions are studied as brain functions is far more powerful."

A full account of the emotional brain is well beyond the scope
of this book. We do need to know though that it is very
important and powerful. Emotional experiences often gain
a privileged status in our memory. The amygdala is
involved in mediating aspects of emotional learning
and also facilitates memory operations in other
regions of the brain including the hippocampus
and prefrontal cortex. It is easier to reactivate
latent emotional associations.[13] This means having
an emotional connection to positive experiences at work
could be a good thing.

Some other highlights include:

- The way that we generate emotional behaviors have been conserved through many levels of evolution. Meaning the historic drives to survive has an impact on us today.
- Emotions and feelings are different, often have similar instigators and can be influenced using different strategies.
- Layers of complexity exist should you choose to dive down the rabbit hole.

Antonio Damasio shares a challenging situation in *Descartes' Error*.[14] Imagine a situation where you are the owner of a large business and you have the opportunity to meet with a potential new client. This person is the archenemy of your best friend. He would give you valuable business, but you'd risk jeopardizing your friendship. Damasio suggests there are at least two distinct ways you can process the quandary. The first is the "high-reason" view, the commonsense view that assumes that logic will deliver us to the best solution and that to do this emotion must be kept out of the picture. This would turn into a very long and tricky calculation requiring value to be ascribed to various different scenarios in order to evaluate the best option. Our working memory capacity is limited, so you'd need pen and paper. However, the strategy is still scattered with weaknesses.[15]

The other approach is called the "somatic-marker" hypothesis. It suggests that we have an automatic response to options. We may experience a feeling in our body, which, if we pay attention to it, could develop into a valuable guide. In the above example, we may experience a "gut feeling" that signals to us that we should immediately discount the option of doing business with this archenemy. One can still engage the rational decision-making process, but the suggestion is after paying attention to any somatic markers. Somatic markers are feelings generated by emotions, which have been connected, by learning, to predicted future outcomes. Somatic markers are established as a natural part of learning. To ignore them, it could be argued, is as strange as ignoring our experience of gravity.

ANDREA CARTWRIGHT – HR DIRECTOR, SUPERGROUP

I certainly have a firm belief that you need an emotional relationship with the organization you work for. I can make the rational connection that I come to work and I get paid and I can pay my mortgage and I can feed my children and all the other things that I like to do. That is a bit transactional, there needs to be more and actually making emotional connections about connecting with the local community and just doing stuff together, my team were.... they've done a mud run recently, couple of them, we have cakes which means you raise money, we all like eating the cakes, we get sociable round the cake table or in the kitchen making a cup of tea. So it has that cohesive effect and actually benefits from it as well; so it's the other connections that we have with the work place [that] aren't just simply about "come to work, I'll do my task and then I'll go home again". We are not in mills anymore, are we? [...]It's that ongoing connection with the business which is very important.

A simple question can reveal a lot about whether contribution is at the heart of an organization. I asked lots of the people I interviewed how they would describe their culture and received a range of responses. The first part of Neil's answer shows how what the company actually contributes is at the core.

> ### NEIL MORRISON – HR DIRECTOR, RANDOM HOUSE GROUP
>
> The two cultures are 80 percent the same between Penguin and Random House, so it wasn't like Alliance and Boots having researchers and retailers coming together [...] People work in publishing because they are passionate about what they do. No one comes to publishing to get rich; they come because they want to work, they want to publish books. That tends to be in any part of the organization that you go to, in Facilities, in HR, in IT, people love books that is why they are here. It doesn't matter whether it is ebooks or paper books, they love books, and so people bring a lot of passion and a lot of heart into work because they are doing something that they believe in.

One of the key pieces within the contribution concept is that people have to be able to articulate what the company for which they work does. All too often when delivering workshops we ask people what their company does, how would they explain what they do to a seven-year-old? More often than not we get a jargon filled paragraph that most seven-year-olds would turn around and walk off in response to. Just because adults politely smile and respond "oh that sounds interesting" does not mean we are clear on what we're contributing. Going deeper into an organization where there are grass-roots-level employees, who may or may not have been involved in any technical processes of creating a company mission, vision, or value statements, offers an opportunity.

Imagine the potential networking and positioning power behind your whole workforce. How many people work for your organization? Imagine if all of them, when asked what they do, could respond clearly, concisely using words that people understand to emotionally (that's with emotion, not tears) describe what they do as part of the overall organization. How would you feel if at the next dinner you went to you met someone new and asked her what she did and she responded, 'I work as part of a team building a better working world.' Would you want to stay and chat a little more? What if instead she responded, 'I'm an accountant'. This same person works at EY and their website says the former. When you last met an accountant how did they describe what they did? Did you feel a connection between them and their work? Did they seem passionate, engaged, loyal to their organization?

We often ask companies, "What would people say if I asked them what your business does?"

ANDREA CARTWRIGHT, HR DIRECTOR, SUPERGROUP

That is a really interesting question and it's one of the questions I asked when I came here. I went around and I said, "Tell me what the business does," and I got everything from "We make clothes," to "We sell a dream," to "We are in the sex industry, because it's actually about feeling good and feeling sexy and looking fabulous." (I kind of get the connection, I'm not sure maybe people would describe it as being in the sex industry.) I thought, actually I kind of get that and I think we still have got a lot of work in the business to really be clear in our own minds what is the point of what we do. I don't think we've quite captured that so that people can[...] say, this is what we do, in the snapshot sentence, people can see this is what we are about and this is why we exist.

So how do I help people get meaning in their work? Because at the end of day even though I might be the HR director, I'm also part of the big machine that develops, designs, manufactures, gets in to store, and gives customers a great experience in store so that you can go home and buy a dress like this and love it. That is what I do. People say, "Well I'm not part of Design," well I am, and I'm a big part of it. I don't sketch the stuff [...] but I am part of that whole thing that sells a dream and makes people feel good. But I think we've got to help a lot of our employees to make that connection, because if you work in Finance, how do you make that connection? We are lucky here because we've got a product that is very tangible and very exciting and renews itself every six months because we have a new season, and one of the things I have changed here is that we make every effort to give every employee in here, regardless of what they do, a chance to go and look and feel and touch the new product and get really excited. Every time we launch a new season I ring up my husband and I say we are going to need a bigger wardrobe because I want that, and I want that, and that is what is all about isn't it? Because if we are excited about fashion then our customers are going to love it too.

So I certainly have a firm belief that you need an emotional relationship with the organization you work for.

What Are You Selling?

The idea that organizations are selling themselves to their employees, current and future and perhaps even past, is not always one that sits comfortably with people. If you already buy into it or can come along for the ride for a short while then we can explore another interesting body of research. The science of consumer behavior and emotion has been well documented over the years. Insights include:

- fMRI research shows that when people evaluate brands they primarily use emotions (how they feel and experience it) rather than information (what the attributes, features, and facts are).
- Our emotional response to an advert has a greater influence on whether or not we say we intend to buy a product than the content of an ad. (3–1 for television adverts and 2–1 for adverts in print).
- Our positive emotions towards a brand have a greater influence on our loyalty than trust and other judgements based on the brand's attributes.[16]

Think about it – the last time you bought pain relief, what did you get? It takes time to convince people that the supermarket own brand will work just as well as the fancy brands of paracetamol. The active ingredients are the same! Our emotional connection to what we buy into it is powerful. There are lots more insights we can take from this body of research to practically apply to how we do things. For now though, let's move on.

Storytelling

Our brains love stories. We thrive on being taken on a journey where we can connect and see and feel the experience. Every story is different and even within the overarching story of an organization there is huge power in each of the individual employee's stories.

When I was 13 I remember going round to my best friend's house during the summer holidays. We sat on one of their very soft sofas while her big sister sat on the hard coffee table. It was a rare time when she was present with us rather than busy studying. She was talking about how happy she was and excited about life. She'd just done her A-levels and was off to the same university in September as her boyfriend. I remember thinking, "Wow, isn't it great when life excites you."

Three weeks later when I went into school the class was reeling with the news that she was dead. One of the boys lived down her road and said there were lots of cars going back and forth. I didn't believe him. It just seemed so wrong. How could this have happened, this wasn't supposed to happen, she was meant to go and have an amazing time at uni and make new friends and touch more people's lives. She was a really warm character with a beautiful smile.

That night I went to my friend's house and just sat with the rawness that the family were experiencing. The days, weeks and years that followed were understandably hard. The funeral was something I'll always remember. Our local church was a converted barn – it could seat over 300 people in the main area, and that wasn't anywhere near enough. People stood spilling out of the doors, all come to honor and say goodbye to this wonderful person.

The contribution she made in 18 years connected with so many people, it was inspirational. As I look back I believe that I "got" quite early on, that this one life we have should be treated as a gift. Each day won't happen again, and you never know which will be your last.

AMY MCKEOWN - HEALTH, MENTAL
HEALTH AND WELL-BEING, EY

A big part of what we did was sharing our stories. After I had developed the mental health agenda at EY and people were comfortable I asked people to share their stories and a lot of people felt that it was safe (and often healing) to disclose theirs. The lady who had postnatal depression wrote us her story on experiencing postnatal depression. That story is now available to our maternity coaches. I have trained them up on postnatal depression and in addition they have got a personal story from someone. We have just redone our maternity policy in terms of paternity, and we also now put postnatal depression stuff in there. So a lot of what we are doing is weaving things into one another and reinforcing.

You may or may not have had personal experience of the power of stories. Here is some of the scientific argument for using them.

The Neuroscience of Storytelling

Cognitive science recognizes narrative as a basic organizing principle of memory. We know from Elizabeth Loftus's work that our minds invent things that never happened, and at times this is to hold the narrative we've told ourselves together.[17] Our need to make stories out of our experiences is strong. In organizations you have probably observed times when two people are remembering something quite differently. It has been shown through experiments with split-brain patients (people in whom the corpus callosum connecting the right and left hemispheres is to some degree severed) that we have an interpreter in residence. In the left hemisphere there is a function that makes sense of memories if it doesn't have access to the memories or context in which they were made.

Stories have the power to grab our attention and elicit an emotional response. In a recent experiment researchers took blood samples of a group before and after they watched a public service announcement (PSA) from the UK. These included the topics smoking, excessive drinking, speeding, and global warming. They were measuring the change in oxytocin and ACTH (a fast-acting arousal hormone). In individuals where the PSA elicited an increase in both oxytocin and ACTH, people afterwards donated 261 percent more to charity. The ACTH change was correlated with the amount of attention they paid to the story.[18] Our attention is a precious commodity and we give it sparingly, always on the lookout for something more deserving.

In another experiment the researchers dug deep to explore why narratives are persuasive. They set out to measure attention and oxytocin responses as close to real time as they could. Even the most captivating stories hold our attention, then we pull away, and then we're pulled back. In this scenario the effectiveness of the narrative was assessed by the donations made afterwards to a linked charity. The authors say they can predict whether a participant would donate money with 82 percent accuracy by measuring the peripheral nervous system's response to the story.[19]

One of the main goals with stories is to invite people into the narrative. "Transportation" is a trademark of an effective story.[20] Stories that affect our behavior, be that contributing to charity or something else, connect with us. Organizations telling *their* story naturally are almost just waiting to be told and to include the people who are already a real part of that story.

Why Do People Need to Be Able to Clearly, Simply and Concisely Articulate What Their Organization Does?

There are several reasons people need to be able to articulate what their organization does. They need to be able to:

• Picture it – being able to explain it clearly increases the likelihood they have a clear picture in their mind.
• Emotionally connect with it.
• Share it.
• Adapt it – to enable others to transport into it.

Potential Pitfalls

Doing it to Check a Box

Many individuals within organizations are overstretched. They have a list of things they need to work through, one of which may be sorting out the company's purpose. Writing a purpose statement is not the same as what we're talking about doing here and will not provide the same benefits.

Engaged with the Cause or the Cause and Vehicle?

People who work for organizations where they believe in what they are doing, quite common in the third sector, often score highly on engage-ment questionnaires. Further exploration may be needed to assess whether this engagement is with the cause or the organization.[21]

Doing it Just to See a Financial Return

Unless meticulous in the approach, if the focus isn't on embedding and networking the concept, then important opportunities are often lost.

Corporate Social Responsibility: Joined up Thinking

Corporate social responsibility (CSR) is a hot topic for organizations. It can be done really well, or really badly. When done simply to check a box it can have a negative impact on people and be dismissed as shallow PR.

One of the best examples I've seen recently is within Hyder Consulting. When I walked into the London office I saw some amazing artwork throughout the building. In the reception area I stood staring at one particular creation made out of rubbish. The lady at reception started explaining to me where it came from and what it meant and how she loved the pictures and wished she had one at home. Her passion and connection with both the artwork and the organization was very evident. She was engaged.

MISTI MELVIEW – GROUP HR & COMMUNICATIONS DIRECTOR, HYDER CONSULTING

We design things, bridges, tunnels, buildings, cities, and we work in communities all around the world so one of the thing that we feel is really important is that we want to put something back into the wider community. So [we] might be dealing with, say, the highway agency with building the road, helping design the road, but we want to do more than that and now we know engineers and architects and the others that we work with are [also] pretty passionate about putting something back into society. Sometimes when you are working in the private or the public sector you feel like you are doing something but doesn't feel like it's enough. I previously worked in a company called Westpac, in Australia, which taught me at a fairly young age some of the things that made people feel good, especially in banking. They were doing something to help humanity and you could see how engaged people were and how it helps with their own learning and development when they get involved with a community type project. We provide in terms of the three areas of CSR. We give advice in that area so we have specialists in environment – you can't be advising clients and not actually thinking about that yourself, looking at our carbon fiber footprint and carbon emission, and so on. It's really important to us that we do what we advise our clients about too, but the particular one that I think has really got a lot of involvement is being engaged in charity work, and we let each [of] our regions choose each year the charity. It's not just about giving money, although we do give financial donations, but for us it's more about our people actually being involved with that charity. We look for where charities have very good causes but more where our people can go and do something to really assist. So if you are in our East Asian operation in Hong Kong, or mainland China, some of our people actually go and help build libraries. [...] There are many impoverished areas and parts of China where they don't have sophisticated schools and so we will help design and build the library and then help with those children ... they will then have hopefully better chances to have access to education.

In Manila is my favorite project, I've visited several times now. Several years ago an English woman called Jane Walker was on holiday and she visited an area where they had the dumpsites and saw these children who were working on the dumpsite and never went to school. Part of the reason they didn't go to school was that they needed to collect rubbish all day that will then earn a little bit of money; they couldn't not do that and take time out to go to school. So she had this brilliant concept of designing a school and she stayed on from her holiday and helped design a school for those children in the dumpsite. She got some land, because this is a capitalist country she had some land donated to her to build this school and somebody donated all those containers that she needed, and she put them together and made a school out of containers. Actually designing a building from containers isn't as easy you might think, because you try to cut out a window or a door in a container and it will sort of implode, and so somebody suggested she come to us because we had very clever designers there and they designed the school. So this wonderful school that houses 1000 children, we helped design and have it built and we've since donated to the school, so we pay for a class for each year and we do a lot of other things in the school.

In addition, we commission the children's artwork, which they make using rubbish from the dumpsite, they make it into this wonderful art and we hang it on our walls. Our people just continued to be involved, so when there was the really bad storms many families lost their homes throughout the Philippines, we've really pulled together across the world and we send clothes, we send gumboots, and all sorts of things. I think that what happens is that our people grow and learn and develop by seeing that we've got over 500 people working in our Manila operation. We are actually one of the biggest employers, if not the biggest British-based employer there and we want to put something back. To me it is the most wonderful example of a truly sustainable type of organization and we've been lucky enough to be involved with them. Really, people feel really fortunate to be involved.

We usually run every one to two years an employee engagement survey and we wanted to increase, as you always do, participation. So a few years ago we said that for every survey that an employee completes we would donate to the school. It's not just something in it for them, obviously we tried to make people understand that it is anonymous and we really need their feedback, but that extra incentive we found did make a difference, we went from rates that were about 70 percent and we went right up to the late 70s by doing that. The other thing we do is online client surveys about how we are working in the project and about our performance with our clients. We also say to our clients if they fill in a survey we'll give to the school.

So we try to connect. I think that if I can get anything across to you with all the different things we do, because I ran HR and Communications, I am able to see how it goes, so that things can work together; I will put my communications hat or my marketing hat or I will put my HR hat on, and I think that helps. If you don't have that in your organization then you need your marketing and coms people and your HR people to work really effectively together and not in conflict, which I have seen elsewhere, so get in line with each other and collaborate, because you can come up with some really interesting ways of looking at it. Give it a go, what have you got to lose? We had everything to gain there and we certainly hope that just another way to provide support and to show our people its actions speak louder than words.

What Are the Keys to Maximizing the Win-Win from CSR?

- Identify what you do; what is your organization really good at?
- Identify a genuine need within a local community that you are well placed to help with.
- Consider how you can bring people together to do something practical (oxytocin releasing opportunity).
- Consider how things can be project based with clearly defined milestones to achieve (dopamine releasing opportunities).
- Communicate what is going on within the organization to everyone who is part of the organization.
- Give people autonomy, trust, time, and resources to do what they are passionate about.

What's the Bottom Line?

Get clear on what your organization contributes. Help every employee to be clear on their contribution.

What Can I Do Today?

Today you could take some snapshots. First a snapshot of how you see the contribution your organization is making and your contribution to that. Second a snapshot of what others think, perhaps by asking a selection of people. Third a snapshot of how any contribution is being communicated throughout the organization – can you see any inconsistencies that would be an opportunity for improvement?

What Can I Put in Place for the Long Term?

Get a team together to create a "contribution wall." This is a space within your place of work where people can come and post, perhaps using Post-it notes or larger pieces of paper, the things they see their organization contributing. Why do they believe their organization deserves to exist? What good do they see it doing?

What Is the Overall Ideal Vision?

The overall vision is for people to be inspired and passion-ate about their work. Overall, when they think about work it activates the reward centers in their brain and they get that warm-glow because they feel proud to be a part of what they are collectively doing.

5 The Jarring Awakening

chapter

I've worked in really different sorts of organizations over the last 30 years and [...] the thing that I'm seeing more and more, and it troubles me, is how stressed people are, how exhausted – so much worrying because of everything you've not done – and how much time they spend connected. The part that I am really interested in at the moment, and what I'm working really closely with my coaching clients in particular, are simple things around being mindful and getting them to switch off and to stop doing things; to be able to plan what they do and concentrate on things; rather than trying to be everything to everyone, to be connected at every hour of the day and night and creating very, very unhealthy lives for themselves. What I'm working now on is using different techniques with them to get them to stop.

One of my coaching clients, she was so stressed when I took her on, I needed to find something really quickly for her and I started investigating apps, because I love technology and I think that is great, in its place. There are some great apps and I've tried them all out and found Headspace; I've got her to use Headspace and in the process of testing out a number of different things I've now become an avid user and it's fantastic!

I've got my headphones with me, in a car park, on a plane, and I can just take 10–20 minutes and stop. I also have a rule at home, which I'm trying to enforce: a digital detox day on Sunday, so that all of us just for a bit, stop, no texting ... I love technology and it's fantastic and a brilliant part of what we do, but I'm concerned that people don't know how to stop and just be present in their lives [...] I've just started on that. I'm really interested and excited by that.

The jarring awakening is that, from one perspective, our brains are incredibly easily influenced. This means that for many of us, we have a lot more opportunity than perhaps was previously thought. We know from Chapter 3 that our brains can and do change. The reason we need to be jarred awake is that most people do not intentionally invest in the shaping of their brains. The opportunity here is to understand some of the ways we know we can help it to wire to assist us to more easily do the things we want, to also become more psychologically flexible.

most people do not intentionally invest in the shaping of their brains

Organizations need the jarring awakening because they are often unintentionally shaping employees brains to be less useful both to the company and to them as individuals. People normally start jobs offering a level of engagement. Our natural state as children is to be engaged. We give our full attention to what we are doing. We are consumed and completely present. We have imaginations and demonstrate creativity. We slowly reprogram ourselves to seek shortcuts to feeling good, settling for less because it is quicker or requires less of us. This doesn't have to be the case though.

There are many areas of research that are interesting and useful to us here and we will focus on three: flow, mindfulness, and mind wandering.

Remember as you go through this chapter the underlying principle is that we can intentionally shape our brains. If you hear people saying that everyone should be in flow more or should be mindful more, that isn't the core message here.

Flow

Dean Potter is great at many sports, including BASE jumping. One of his jumps gives us some powerful insights into this state. He was jumping into the Cellar of Swallows in Mexico. This is a 1200 feet deep open air pit filled with around 50,000 swifts. Potter and his friends had been jumping into the cave all weekend and were all pretty exhausted. He said afterwards that he had been feeling sick for almost a day, he was exhausted, he had a bad feeling in his gut, and he ignored all of this and did one last jump.

It is really important that a parachute is dry. If it is wet then it is asymmetrical when deployed. Potter's was wet. He ignored it. Potter recalls that when he leapt into the cave he immediately got into the zone and all his sense started to peak. Despite moving at 90 miles per hour he could see things in incredible detail. He noted the minute fissures in the rock and tiny patches of lichen and bat guano. This heightened visual capacity was going to become very useful shortly.

When he was about 500 feet from the ground he deployed his parachute. It opened asymmetrically which meant that he started spinning. His guidelines were twisted, so steering became impossible. His friends safely above him started shouting, "Avoid the walls!"

Amazingly the guidelines began to untwist. He yanked the toggles and turned so he was heading directly towards a cave wall. As he turned, the parachute collapsed over his head. His senses continued to peak and just before his vision was completely obscured he saw a glimpse of orange. This orange was a rope for the camera man. Immediately Potter reacted and grabbed and caught the rope. The friction burnt through his flesh. He was in agony but held on. He brought himself to a stop, parachute still over his head, just six feet from the floor. His friends shouted, "Just let go!"

Many athletes, like Potter, enter into the state of flow on a daily basis. With time it becomes easier to get into the state quickly. Staying in that state of flow probably saved Potter's life that day. Things moving in super slow motion, being able to hear his friend's instructions, process them and make decisions all made a huge difference.

Let's rewind to the beginning and check in on the psychological understanding of flow first. In Mihaly Csikszentmihalyi's pivotal book, *Flow*, he describes optimal experience as something that we *make* happen.[1] Flow "provides a sense of discovery, a creative feeling of transporting a person into a new reality. It pushes a person to higher levels of performance and leads to previously undreamed of states of consciousness." In this amazing state we experience pleasure, wellbeing, and increased cognitive efficiency. We are completely absorbed in the task at hand; in the zone. There are many conditions that make it more likely for us to enter into a state of flow that Mihaly initially outlined and which have since been further explored by people.[2] In Part IV we develop the practical applications of this information into how to manage to create opportunities.

Intensely Focused Attention

One of the keys to experiencing flow is a long period of uninterrupted concentration. A deep focus needs to be allowed to materialize. When we reflect on a typical day we might notice how rare these times are for many of us. Most people say they get far more done when they create these times, often by working from an empty home. People say they get to a place of deep embodiment when in flow. They merge with the task. All their senses become heightened and time slows down. This takes serious concentration so the removal of distractions or ability to block them out is really key.

Clear Goals

It has been identified that clarity in what you're doing and why you're doing it is important. You want to be present in the moment and what you're doing. For many people who practice what appears, to a novice, to be the same thing time after time, hour after hour, day after day, there are actually very clear minute distinctions. For the golfer who practices putt after putt he may be focusing on creating a curve or controlling his velocity or the little finger's position within his hand grip. Improving each tiny distinction both helps make them among the best and also enables them to experience flow on a daily basis.

Immediate Feedback

The wonderful thing about having clear goals is that it is easier for the brain to process feedback. The feedback helps us focus and refine what we do next. It means our brain isn't searching for how to improve. Of course it is easier to identify the feedback if we have clear goals.

Challenge/Skills Ratio

The state of flow is often seen when there is a good match between the challenge of a task and the skill level of the person performing it. The task can't be too dull because our attention disengages and our action and awareness can't merge. However, nor can the task be too hard because our fear levels increase and we can want to stop. Tasks should be like Goldilocks – just right. People enjoying various activities, including rock climbing, jazz improvisation, chess, and performing surgery, all report entering into flow when the challenge to skills ratio was right.

Sense of Control

Autonomy over what you are doing is important. You want to feel competent, yet stretched; in control, yet perhaps that there are other factors also at play. Kotler suggests that risk can be a trigger to getting into flow.[2] This is seen obviously in extreme sports enthusiasts where their lives are risked each time they enjoy their sport. A subtler version is perhaps seen in musicians (the challenge of risking a mistake and a damaged reputation) or at work (getting it wrong).

Rich Environment

Knowing that our environment influences us greatly choosing one that offers novelty, unpredictability, and complexity could be a double-edged sword. The intention is for these components to catch and focus the attention. The risk is that they distract from the task.

All the conditions are linked. We talk about them using language that is imperfect and lose some of the core truth that underpins the experience. However soon we will look at the neural correlates of flow.

Before that it is useful to note that we've been talking about flow as a very personal, individual state until now. While it absolutely is, it can also be experienced in groups. We will explore this further in Chapter 8. So what does it feel like to experience flow?

1. An intense and focused concentration on the present moment
2. The merging of actions and awareness
3. A loss of reflective self-consciousness
4. A sense of personal control over the situation
5. Temporal distortion (normally time slowing down)
6. The experience is intrinsically rewarding.[3]

The Brain Waves of Flow

To process information we have evolved two distinct systems. The descriptions of these systems are often overlapped or muddled with others. Keeping it simple, let's consider the explicit system, which involves the prefrontal cortex. This is that rule-based system that we're normally consciously aware of ticking away. It is logical, rational, and energy intensive to run. The other system is the implicit system. It is mostly below the level of conscious awareness and involves the basal ganglia. Sometimes described as our intuition, gut feel, and normally difficult to explain. It relies on our skills and experience.[4]

Consider a master chess player, which Csikszentmihalyi and others have done over the years. Electroencephalogram (EEG) has been used to see what networks in the brain are active. Chess is clearly a game of reasoning, planning, and strategy – all things the prefrontal cortex is involved in. Beta activity would be expected. However, chess masters are not alone in using their implicit system, denoted by a low alpha and high theta wave activity, driving their decisions while in flow in their field of expertise.

When sharing this research with organizations it is often challenging for people to understand just how much we are driven to transition processes from the explicit to the implicit system. As David Eagleman shares, "When the brain finds a task it needs to solve it rewires its own circuitry until it can accomplish this task with maximum efficiency. The task becomes burned into the machinery…"[5] By automating things we enable fast decisions to be made. Having to consciously process information in your working memory slows things down. We used to have to make quick decisions because our lives depended on it. That is less likely to be the case for most people today, however we are still more efficient if we harness the power of the implicit system. Of course the quality of the decisions depends on the quality of the input. Trusting instinct is less useful in assessing a stock if you've never looked at any before.

Chess players have invested years in learning patterns and move sequences, which mean that they have a high quality of information stored within their brains. Their implicit system can be trusted to guide them to winning moves without their explicit cognitive system needing to expend costly energy in assessing the board.

So what is actually going on when we are trying to make decisions in flow? Rather than flow being a switch that is turned on and off it is understood from the data that people move through a cycle. Initially we're in a baseline state before a novel stimulus arises. From there we go through problem solving, pre-action readiness, action, post-action evaluation, and then circle back to baseline. Each of these stages is important. Each of these stages involves different parts of the brain and produces different brain waves. Experts can create, control, and move through these states.

To get into and remain in a state of flow, mental control is important. Being able to shut off distractions and even turn down the explicit system – no easy feat for most executives – is the holy grail. Most people have done this without the aid of technology, although now neuro-feed-back is becoming more popular and with proper implementation could help more people finetune their responses.[6]

The elusive "Aha!" moment is much sought after (the process of which often chases it further away). Thirty milliseconds before that moment, EEG shows a burst of gamma waves. This happens when widely distributed cells, typically novel stimuli, random thoughts, and ambiguous memories connect together. Gamma spikes always occur within theta oscillations. (Theta processes novel incoming stimuli so this makes sense.) Many experienced meditators, after a lot of practice, can control theta waves. People who are already in flow will have low alpha wave high theta wave patterns and so are primed ready for that gamma spike. This is the state that is primed for creative decision making.[2]

The Revelation of Flow

When we think about thinking, we first (and often only) consider the type of conscious thinking that the prefrontal cortex is involved in. It enables us to plan ahead, solve problems, assess risk, evaluate rewards, suppress urges, learn from experience, and analyze and essentially is at the core of our cognitive processing. Surely better thinking means a better, more active prefrontal cortex? Evidently not. Instead transient hypo-frontality is noted, that is slow front brain (where the prefrontal cortex is housed). The energy that is saved from running this hungry part of the brain is redirected to increase our attention and awareness.

Remember that "loss of self" feeling associated with flow? Well, the superior frontal gyrus is involved in creating that introspective feeling and its deactivation enables us to not be distracted by how we feel about something. We appear to be able to switch on and off this self-awareness.[7] At times, not being caught up in self-analysis can make a big difference on speed and efficiency.

A special keyboard was designed to be used in an fMRI scanner to enable us to understand what happens when jazz musicians improvise. It was discovered the inhibition and self-censoring is turned down (the dorso-lateral prefrontal cortex) and self-expression and creativity is turned up (the medial prefrontal cortex).[8] Talented jazz musicians create music that has never been heard before. Some organizations would love people to generate new ideas, competitively advantageous ways of doing things, and to have creative insights.

In the depths of flow, people share that they ascend to a higher level of consciousness. They have clarity, intuition, and focus and feel part of their environment. Some even describe it as a psychic connection to the universe. Research looking at the brains of meditating Buddhist monks and praying Franciscan nuns showed very low activity in the posterior superior parietal lobe. This part of the brain (the orientation association area) helps us orient our body in physical space. The experience, as neuroscientists would mostly predict, has a neural correlate. The energy that normally helps us identify where we end and the rest of the world begins is saved.

The revelation of flow is that less is more. Less areas of the brain are using up energy enabling it to be directed in a focused way to that which we are focusing on. This creates much more focus than we normally are afforded. The power of this enables people to stand out from the crowd and achieve impressive things.

Quality Thinking

We have become conditioned to believe that quality thinking needs to be laborious. If a team member went out for a long walk in the middle of the morning and when questioned replied that they've been doing some great thinking, would they be commended? When was the last time you held a meeting in a local museum? Or wood? Or golf course?

Our brain is always processing. We have expectations wired into us and when those expectations are met we're rewarded with a little dose of dopamine. When the expectations are not met we are prompted to pay attention.[9] We may or may not listen and respond to this prompt. People often report that they "had a funny feeling" about something and wished they had investigated further.

When dopamine is released it helps us learn new patterns, increases our attention, reduces noise in neural networks, and makes it easier for us to notice more patterns. We are then primed to register further patterns. So our insights are set up to snowball. We can experience dopamine as excitement, engagement, creativity, and drive. It is released when something is novel or when we are exploring something. You'll remember from Chapter 3 on how we learn that neurons that fire together, wire together. We build up our neural network piece by piece to enable us to see things more quickly next time. We can improve our ability to notice things, to have insights and to do whatever we want to do better. Just like you can build a train track to take you from A to B directly, so can you wire your brain to help you make that journey most efficiently too.

you wire your brain to help you make that journey

Norepinephrine speeds up our heart rate, muscle tension, respiration, and tells our body to release more glucose so we have energy. In the brain it also increases attention, arousal, neural efficiency, and emotional control. It helps us stay focused with enough energy.

A lot of research has been done into the state of flow during exercise. Less so, in other triggers of flow, such as at work. There is expected to be more overlaps. We know that endorphins and anandamide are released during exercise-induced flow. Anadamide (an endogenous cannabinoid) elevates mood, relieves pain, aids respiration, and amplifies lateral thinking. It can even inhibit fear.

Towards the end of a flow cycle serotonin is released. All in all, the chemical cocktail that underpins the experience of flow is a very compelling one. It is no surprise that people who experience it are driven to replicate the experience.

Fight or Flight and Flow

The way that the brain works means that when we hear something vaguely familiar, we often link a new concept to an old one. This may or may not be an appropriate link. In neuroscience there is so much to digest and so many foundations to build confusion is commonplace. The fight or flight response is different to the state of flow, although there are links. When reading that the flow state is a compelling one some people jump to the image of an "adrenaline junkie." However, sports people report transitioning from the fight or flight experience into flow. A risky situation can increase our focus and awareness. The familiar adrenaline rush (which also includes norepinephrine) does focus us but the extreme survival autopilot where there are two (or three if you include freezing) options is limiting. Flow increases our flexibility, and in this problem-solving state creativity is prevalent. When chemically primed for flow, it is possible to progress into this useful state or remain in the fight or flight zone, sometimes with unfortunate consequences.

In flow, there isn't the need for the fight or flight response. When the implicit system has the information it needs to enable the explicit system to turn down and trust, then impressive performance can follow.

Mindfulness

Mindfulness is very topical currently and has an interesting body of neuroscientific research behind it. Being mindful isn't new. The concept of "intentional, accepting and non-judgemental focus of one's attention on the emotions, thoughts and sensations occurring in the present moment"[10] is a natural one. Rob Narin defines it as "knowing what is happening, as it happens, whatever it is." Most children are excellent at being mindful and present. Mindfulness can be practiced informally in whatever we are doing. We can make a cup of tea mindfully, speak with a colleague mindfully, reply to emails mindfully. You could, probably with a lot of practice, go through your workday being mindful.

The practice of mindfulness meditation has gained a lot of attention over recent years. When we work with organizations it often surprises me that it is frequently misunderstood. The state of mindfulness and the meditative practice are different, linked but different. Let's first look at the business case for paying attention. A study looked at correlations between the mindfulness of individuals at work and their engagement, energy level, and dedication at work. The managers were also asked to rate the individual's job performance. The researchers found that those with higher mindfulness scores also received better job performance assessments from their managers.[11]

higher mindfulness scores also received better job performance

Mindfulness has been linked to:[12]

* People being more aware of their unconscious processes.
* People having more cognitive control.
* People having a greater ability to shape what they do and say.

John Teasdale once said,[13]

> Mindfulness is a habit, it's something the more one does, the more likely one is to be in that mode with less and less effort … it's a skill that can be learned. It's accessing something we already have. Mindfulness isn't difficult. What's difficult is to remember to be mindful.

How Does It Work?

Essentially there are two distinct forms of self-awareness, two different ways we interact with the world. There appears to be a "fundamental neural dissociation between two distinct forms of self-awareness that are habitually integrated but can be dissociated through attentional training: the self across time and in the present moment."[14]

One is the default mode network (DMN), which includes parts of the medial prefrontal cortex and hippocampus. This network typically becomes active when we're not focused on something external, sometimes referred to as being in a task-absent state. It may be that we start to think about ourselves, envisioning the future, retrieving memories, or gauging others' perspectives.[15] When we start daydreaming, perhaps at our desk, writing has paused and we're imagining a big Tuna Niçoise salad for lunch and planning how we'd make it – this would be the default mode network at work. It would also be active when you start weaving related information together. The DMN involves parts of the medial temporal lobe, medial prefrontal cortex, posterior cingulate cortex, ventral precuneus, and parietal cortex. Its structure and functional connectivity is very overlapped making it easy for the network to be active as long as we're not involved in some other focused task.

The DMN is active for most of our waking hours and doesn't require much effort to work. You can think of it as the operator of our internal narrative. Interestingly, there isn't much evidence of this network in children. Connectivity is starting to be seen around ages 9–12 years. This suggests the network develops. If children aren't processing the world through the DMN, then how are they?

The other network that enables us to interact with the world is the one that is active when we have an experiential focus. It appears that this is better developed in people who practice mindfulness. This experiential focus involved the lateral prefrontal cortex, insula, secondary somatosensory cortex and inferior parietal lobule. The functional connectivity between the right insula and medial prefrontal cortex was strongly coupled in novices of mindfulness but uncoupled in people who practiced mindfulness. The suggestion is that there the two forms of self-awareness are habitually integrated but can be dissociated through attentional training such as mindfulness.[14]

Power of Mindfulness

Mindfulness, and meditation in general has for centuries been thought to influence the interactions between sensory, cognitive, and affective processes. Meditation allows a non-evaluative representation of sensory events. This can be seen clearly in experiments that subject volunteers to pain. People who have been trained in mindfulness mediation (for as little as four days) who then meditated while experiencing pain showed a reduction in perception of unpleasantness by 57 percent and pain intensity by 40 percent compared to rest. Pain-related activation of the contralateral primary somatosensory cortex was reduced. The reduced intensity ratings were associated with increased activity in the anterior cingulate cortex and anterior insula. These areas are involved in cognitive regulation of nociceptive processing. The unpleasantness reductions were associated with orbitofrontal cortex activation. This area is involved in reframing the contextual evaluation of sensory events. Additionally the reduction in pain unpleasantness was also associated with thalamic deactivation. This may mean there is a limbic gating mechanism involved in modifying interactions between afferent input and our executive brain areas.[16]

What Does This All Tell Us?

RAFFAELA GOODBY – HEAD OF OD, ENGAGEMENT AND WELL BEING, BIRMINGHAM CITY COUNCIL

A lot of the messages people get are about cuts; we've got to find £125 million in savings. There are all sorts of things going on in the press. How people feel about their work, they will naturally be feeling under pressure.

We have been trialing Mental Health First Aid, trying to put it in the same place as "breaking your leg" First Aid. We've also really pushed the Time To Change pledge around positive mental health. We had a big event where we signed the Time To Change pledge. All the events where we spoke to big groups of staff we talked also about Time To Change and the sort of resources that were available and having that mental health conversation in your team. 23 percent of our sickness is related to anxiety and stress or depression. So it is a key financial and organizational driver.

Each of our BEST leaders are given two actions related to Time To Change each year. One of their actions is either to have a conversation about mental health in their teams (using the guidance they've been given – packs, videos, badges). Or generally to make a pledge to do something like phoning a friend with depression or looking up bipolar disorder, or I will go on some training about how to approach conversations with people with mental health issues. There are hundreds and hundreds of pledges you can make. It is to get people talking about mental health. It is a key issue for us.

Often at work we feel hurt, it rarely is from a physical pain though. This experiment, along with many others, shares the insight that the brain can be more effectively wired to deal with pain. If we're able to cushion against some of the negative experiences we have at work, we are likely to remain more engaged. Our relationship with an organization is such a delicate thing. It is so easily unintentionally negatively influenced. They say people leave managers rather than jobs.

Meditation engages multiple brain mechanisms and these have the power to alter the subjective experience from afferent information. Our brains can make things feel less bad.

One in four people will experience some kind of mental health problem in the course of a year.[17] In the UK, mixed anxiety and depression is the most common mental disorder. Many organizations are now accessing something called "Mental Health First Aid.". They are training their people to become "mentors" or "leaders" on a mental health first aid basis within their organizations. People are taught how to spot the early signs of a mental health problem.

AMY MCKEOWN – HEALTH, EY

We consider the prevention aspect of Thinking Differently to be Mental Health First Aid. You could perhaps argue the semantics of whether it is prevention or cure. Practically it covers stress as a precursor to mental illness but the program also covers depression, anxiety, panic attacks, bipolar, psychosis, eating disorders, suicide, and OCD, so it is very encompassing. I like the language – Mental Health First Aid – because what you're always wary of when you're doing something around mental health is that you alienate 99% of the workforce who don't think it is for them. So our health, mental health, and wellbeing approach is about getting everyone involved. Mental Health First Aid (MHFA) has the same language as First Aid (physical) so there is an argument that everyone in the company should do it because actually it is the same as doing a Red Cross course. This helped me get engagement.

MHFA is about explaining what these things are and also what they are not. It is also about First Aid so how you are aware of other people and how to support them. So we regard it as a life skill and encourage as many people as possible to do it. We offer a two-day course which we bespoked to include our own case studies and our own internal sources of support. We have also run two-hour courses, which some parts of the business have chosen to make mandatory. As a firm we have a counsellor network because we are project based and so it is easy to not have any permanent line manager. Your counsellor is responsible for your pastoral care and also your representative at round tables and end of year, etc. New Counsellor training is one day and comes from the global company. We have just launched a second day which is mandatory for all counsellors and we have an hour of the Mental Health First Aid training in there. We focus the day on conversations that you are having with your employee. Poor performance can often be a mental health issue in disguise. How do you open up a conversation with your employees around that? It's about awareness raising.

After a year we've had hundreds of people go through it. People sign up within a day and all 100 new places have been snapped up. It is a piece that external press seem to pick up on. Other firms come to us about this and the buddy network. They seem to have struck a chord.

Mindfulness-based interventions have been very effective in reducing the recurrence of depressive symptoms, anxiety, and stress.[18] They have also reduced the risk of relapse in people who have had at least three previous incidents of depression by 43 percent.[19] It is thought that the non-reactivity to inner experience component of mindfulness that really protects people who practice it from the psychological risk for depression. Mindfulness can help reduce people's vulnerability to depression by buffering against both trait rumination and negative bias and also by reducing the automatic emotional responses via the insula.[20]

Bold Suggestion

Let's start investing in DNA-level changes – literally rather than figuratively. A review of seven wellbeing programs suggested the average benefit–cost ratio was a recovery of £4.17 for every £1 spent.[21] That's fantastic. The next stage though is organizations having brain health and strength at the core of how they do things. All things. Maybe it doesn't make any sense to have the entire organization invited to join a wellbeing program where they are encouraged to exercise, maybe lose weight, certainly eat well, and then to have biscuits in every staff meeting. Consistency is key. While we will always need First Aid for physical and mental health, let's consider how we can have more health and safety in place so we fall back on the First Aid less and less. Everything that is happening within an organization has the potential to be shaping employees brains. Much of what goes on just happens without consideration for the effect it could be having on people.

Anxious, Who Me?

Anxiety is common. It can be thought of as the cognitive state related to our inability to control emotional responses to perceived threats. Subsequently it becomes obvious to consider the brain activity associated with our cognitive regulation of emotions. A study compared what happens when people did mindfulness meditation (after training) versus attending to the breath (ATB; before mindfulness training). It found that ATB did not reduce state anxiety, but mindfulness did. The MRI scans showed that anterior cingulate cortex, ventromedial prefrontal cortex, and anterior insula were all activated. Mindfulness helps reduce anxiety by helping to regulate self-referential thought processes.[22]

So we know that mindfulness training helps to modulate the areas of the brain (anterior cingulate cortex and insula) which are important for attentional control, emotional regulation, and interoception. It would be fair to say that military personnel are likely to experience stressful environments, and this puts them at risk of cognitive, emotional, and physiological compromise. Therefore they are a great group to experiment with mindfulness. One study looked at whether training in mindfulness modulated neural processing of interoceptive distress in a group of marines prior to deployment to Afghanistan. If it helped them it could probably help in most organizations! Half of the marines received 20 hours of mindfulness-based mind fitness training. They found that the trained half demonstrated a significant attenuation of right anterior insula and anterior cingulate cortex when exposed to an aversive stimulus. It was concluded that mindfulness training may help modulate the brain's response to negative interoceptive stimuli, which could help strengthen resilience.[23]

Mindfulness has been compared to an aerobic exercise stress reduction program. People suffering from social anxiety disorder were assigned to one group or the other and it was found that the mindfulness-based stress reduction group experienced greater reductions in negative emotion when implementing regulation and increases in attention-related parietal cortical regions. People reported less negative emotion and lowered social anxiety symptom severity.[24]

Why Wait?

A jarring reality for me is that most organizations are reactive rather than proactive. Shaping employees brains to be stronger, more resilient, fit for purpose is something that starts delivering results from day one. Why is it then that organizations often bring externals in to fix problems rather than lay strong foundations?

Speaking with a gentleman the other day, he said that the company for whom he works impresses many people. He said they are 50 years old, most people think, "Wow – all that experience and knowledge." He followed this in an exasperated tone with, "They're not 50 years old, they're one year old, 50 times!"

While full enlightenment ("an exceptional state of well-being arising from a complete balance of virtuous motivation, attention, wholesome emotions and experiential understanding of the nature of mind"[25]) is not on most organization's wish lists, could we at least think bigger than just solving problems?

Meditation Magic?

There is the concern that organizations hear about the benefits of mindfulness and implement a program expecting amazing results. What we don't know from the outside is how mindful individuals are actually becoming. Is it another check-box initiative without the depth to really see results? This loops us back to the suggestion that a well-considered strategy is one of your most valuable assets. By understanding what you want to achieve as an organization, then getting clear on what type of brains you need to achieve that, finally putting things in place such as meditation training will get a far better result than the piecemeal approach.

What Else Does the Research Say about Mindfulness?

- Mindfulness has been shown to reduce chocolate cravings by improving people's dis-identification skills.[26]
- It leads to functional connectivity changes between core DMN regions – possibly reflecting strengthened present-moment awareness.[27]

- Long-term meditators have structural differences in both gray and white matter of the brain.[28]
- Different forms of meditation can involve different brain networks and change the brain in different ways. Compassion meditation enhances empathic accuracy and related neural activity.[29]
- An emotion-oriented mediation, such as the loving-kindness meditation has led to an increase in gray matter volume in the right angular and posterior parahippocampal gyri. This has a role in theory of mind and cognitive empathy, anxiety, and mood.[30]
- Mindfulness leads to reductions in perceived stress and rumination.[31]
- Our immune function can be enhanced through mindfulness practice.[32]

These benefits are huge and we've not even touched on decision making, creativity, problem solving, and the avoidance of multi-tasking. The message is not that mindfulness is great for everything, rather that you can intentionally strengthen your internal processing. If your role, or members of your team's roles involve quality decision making then mindfulness techniques have been shown to have a positive effect on all the widely recognized stages of the decision-making process.[33] The opportunity is to start considering what brain you need for your role and how you can further strengthen yourself in that direction.

you can intentionally strengthen your internal processing

Some of these points may feel a little jarring when your brain naturally starts to ask – so what? What am I supposed to do now? Ask yourself, what do my people need? The ability to focus more? To regulate their emotional responses? To reduce their stress levels? Starting with the end in mind is essential to crafting next steps that actually deliver results for everyone.

Reflect and explore where the workforce is currently at. Do you think most people spend a lot of time utilizing their default mode network? Is there evidence that the network that enables them to be present is strong? Do you think people are easily able to get into a state of hypofrontality?

Our vision for the future includes both organizations doing great work and the companies supporting those organizations all understanding how what they are or aren't doing actually works. Science isn't everything, but it is a very useful, under-utilized piece.

Nurture is our piece around cure. It's obviously a big and very important issue for us, if people are sick we want them to get back to health and work quickly. Our aim is to do the best for the health and mental health of our staff and make everyone happier. There is also another piece we should consider. We pay a lot for people to join our organization, we then pay them pretty high salaries, and we spend a lot on training them; so if they are absent then that makes a difference to our bottom line. Absence costs us a huge amount of money.

People don't think of health care costs in that way. They think about how much we pay for private health insurance not how much we're losing in absence.

What's the Bottom Line?

Brains can be, and are being, shaped. Intentionally:

Decide – what qualities you want from your brains.
Design – the experiences that will shape those brains.
Create – the environments that will encourage those experiences.

What Can I Do Today?

Decide, design, create – if not for your whole organization then at least for yourself. Become a shining example of someone intentionally shaping your brain to perform at your best. Examples of things that will benefit most people include:

Do some exercise today and push yourself further than you have before.

Choose to give yourself a breathing space. Just one minute to stop doing, and be. Breathe.

Consider, how often do you just be? Do you connect with your environment and feel your feelings, see what is in front of you, and allow your thoughts to pass without judgement?

What Can I Put in Place for the Long Term?

Create opportunities for people to learn about the state of flow, the effect of meditation on their brain, and how to have more of them in their life.

Train Brain Ambassadors and Brain Buddies to filter information out to help strengthen the work force, and help people be responsible and accountable for their own brain shaping.

Having the shaping of people's brains firmly on the radar of strategic discussions. Top-level decisions filter down to affect employees which then affects performance.

What Is the Overall Ideal Vision?

An organization whose environment, policies, systems, and culture are supporting the type of brains you want people to have to be fulfilled doing their best work.

6
chapter

The Reassuring Truth

The reassuring truth is that we are wired for interpersonal attachments. This is a fundamental human motivation.[1] It is incredibly powerful. It is that power that is reassuring. We need frequent interactions with people with whom we have an ongoing bond. Feeling that you belong somewhere, with some people, has multiple strong effects on emotional patterns and cognitive processes. A lack of attachment causes pain, increases our perception of stress, impairs cognitive functioning, and can interfere with the immune response.

There are many angles and opportunities to be evaluated within this chapter. We start with the most obvious, hoping that experientially it makes a lot of sense to you. From there we navigate the concepts that should feature in high-level strategic discussions in order to support a workforce that both performs at its best and enjoys that process.

The Price of a Lack of Connection

Imagine you have joined a new organization. You're really excited about this fresh start and are keen to give a lot to this place as you build your career here. All this engagement and motivation is present in bucket loads and is on offer for the organization to benefit from. These first days, weeks, and months are incredibly shaping. Emotions are running high, expectations are primed, and friends and family will be asking how the new job is going. What would someone say after a few days at your place of employment?

What would people say after a few months?

Loneliness as a form of social pain has been shown to activate the dorsal anterior cingulate. This is the same area of the brain that registers emotional responses to physical pain.[2] Cacciopo and Patrick share three complex factors they believe input into the powerful effects of loneliness:[3]

1. Level of vulnerability to social disconnection
2. Ability to self-regulate the emotions associated with feeling isolated
3. Mental representations and expectations of, as well as reasoning about, others.

There are some factors we can do something about (numbers two and three). Chapters 3 and 5 give insights into how we can do something about our ability to self-regulate. In this chapter, we will make some suggestions about how you can strengthen the organization's culture and practices to influence people's expectations and experiences.

The big opportunity is that many organizations are not putting a solid understanding of this reassuring truth at the center of how they work. Everything from building design, the way meetings are conducted, the things people are measured on and rewarded for, to the existing culture could be having a positive or negative influence on how *connected* people are.

In most organizations people typically come together with others, in a variety of different ways, on a regular basis when working. Is this enough though? What about when you don't even get to see colleagues? One of the biggest challenges a close friend of mine has, as a locuming GP, is that by moving from workplace to workplace she doesn't regularly see anyone she has bonds with. She goes into a practice for a day, doesn't know anyone, often doesn't get to see any other doctors or nurses or receptionists, sees many patients, and then leaves. While the friendly face at the start of the day from the welcoming receptionist (sometimes) is great – it isn't enough to last all day. Most people do not share this situation, but increasing numbers of people may not see colleagues all day. There are things that can be done.

Feeling alone often doesn't have to mean that there are no people around. It is possible to feel completely isolated while being surrounded by others in hustle and bustle. Sometimes the culture doesn't value connecting with people, and subsequently people focus on getting the job done, to the detriment of building real relationships.

It is possible to feel completely isolated while being surrounded

This chapter goes beyond what would normally be considered under the topic of connection. That is one of the benefits of neuroscience; we can take lateral steps and then draw relevant links. The result is that we have a broader understanding and more flexible options to move forward. We will examine:

- Connection before communicating – improving efficiency and effectiveness
- The benefits of empathy and how to make it more likely
- Positive empathy specifically and the collaborative potential

What Are Organizations Already Doing?

JANE OLDS – HEAD OF HR, WEATHERBYS

I think that what we did as work in the ground levels, that we have team one-to-ones and team meets, from a companywide perspective we have a weekly internet email that goes out to everybody in the organization, we then have quarterly what we call "Love ins," which is where we bring larger groups of people in our conference center, so in groups of 100, [and] we will basically communicate what is going on in the business and open the floor for people to ask questions about how things are going [...] and feel that they have a voice in things that we are doing and looking towards doing in the future. So far, [those are] our main communication tools but we then have other loads of social activities that go on that then encourage more communication amongst the wider team, so we are mixing groups of people together. For example, tonight we've got a barbeque going on and there will be people going from all over the business that [don't] ordinarily crossover so that is quite important to people, finding out about more pockets of the business rather just sitting in their own area and being isolated.

LOUISA FRYER – L&D MANAGER, CATH KIDSON

We've got a social committee that is made up with people around the building, either people that have been here for a long while or people that are new, people from all over the different departments and they basically get together once a month. Last month we had a barbecue on Friday. So we do events like that, but then the girls are also looking at doing other personal pieces that we do up here in the café. So that's a sign of some social event going on. Then the offer that we are working on at the moment links into wellbeing. We've got a masseuse that comes in once a month, we have a lady that does nails, we have yoga and meditation sessions as well.

GRAHAM SALISBURY – HEAD OF HR FOR ACTIONAID UK

Day one of three I had all of my team together so that they can see what each other does: Maria can learn exactly what Victoria does and vice versa, so there is an understanding of each other's roles. Partly just because it's good to know what each of them does, but also there is an aspiration for some of the junior members of the team to progress into more senior HR roles, and you can understand better what they do in that environment. Days two and three were all about how to be an effective business partner, managing conversations, those kind of things. We were being charged for the training for eight seats and got about three people, so spoke to people in other charities, including Fairtrade Foundation, Tearfund, CAFOD, and also People in Aid. In the end, there were four or five organizations. We'd already paid for this and wanted to participate and what that then led to was they were all engaged because it was quite high power stuff. It improved the learning because you are not just hearing how you experience issues within your environment but you can learn from others in real life that there are various ways in which you can improve. I think that the opportunity to share with various other people was great and that then led on to various other things.

The Reassuring Molecule

Oxytocin is a little molecule that has been linked to many positive words. To organizations it can offer reassurance because oxytocin influences social behavior. It can also reduce stress reactivity, increase our tolerance for pain, reduce distractibility, and help retain executive control.

Paul Zak suggests that oxytocin is produced in high-performing workplaces. "If you want to keep people on task all the time, you want oxytocin-producing situations." One way that oxytocin levels are raised in organizations is through trust. It is suggested that trust is a temporary attachment between people. We know that oxytocin levels rise with a social signal of trust and it is associated with trustworthy behavior (when people reciprocate trust).[4] We will look at this further in Chapter 8.

Zak also suggests other ways oxytocin levels can be raised:

- Praise people publicly and unexpectedly.
- Be transparent in identifying tasks and setting goals.
- Delegate work effectively.
- Encourage learning through mistakes.
- Build caring relationships.
- Be empathetic to others.
- Invest in the whole person's growth.
- Be vulnerable.

Assessing how your organization is doing on each of these fronts both overtly and through the more subtle nuances that shape people's behavior could pay dividends.

The Idea Salesperson

In most organizations at various times we need people to help sell ideas to others. It has been found that the best idea salespeople tend to have differences in the neural activity within their temporoparietal junction (TPJ). It is possible this is because the TPJ is associated with considering the mental states of others. It is suggested that the people who engage in more consideration or simulation of other people's viewpoints at the time when they are initially being exposed to an idea, may later be in a better position to successfully communicate these ideas to others.

The next stage to this is to consider social language. This has been linked to multiple positive outcomes from depth of conversational engagement to success in cooperative problem solving.[5,6,7] Social language includes individuals and the interactive processes (for example, *colleague, friend, people, talk, email, share*). Fascinatingly, by using more social language we facilitate social communication.[8] Our social cues in the language we use activates neural systems that are implicated both in understanding the state of others and also then successfully re-transmitting ideas. The mechanisms at work here go beyond semantic priming. The brain is affected by the way ideas are initially shared. This influences how a person goes on to share the idea.

The brain is affected by the way ideas are initially shared

What Does This Mean Practically?

When introducing new ideas, get people together to discuss them in depth. Create an environment where people can freely discuss their thoughts. Consider the state people come to this experience in; this is likely to influence their discussions. Prime people to discuss things using social language. You want people to think about the idea from multiple perspective points, considering how the idea benefits others. Thinking big picture right down to detail and what that means for people and what people do and how they do it.

Keep Your Friends Close, and Your Strangers...?

How we connect with others is linked to how empathetic we are. Interdependence is known to enhance our empathy for people we are already connected to, but at the cost of decreasing our empathy for strangers. When we observe a friend being socially excluded there is a neural response in the medial prefrontal cortex (mPFC) and to a lesser extent the dorsal anterior cingulate cortex (dACC) and anterior insula (AI). On the other hand, when a stranger is experiencing social exclusion we see a negative correlation between interdependence, perspective-taking, and empathic concern and activation of the same brain areas. It is suggested that while individuals who have higher trait interdependence may be better able to empathize, they may exercise this ability primarily for people closer to them.[9]

What Does This Mean Practically?

We need to create opportunities for people to build relationships. The marketing manager will be far better able to step into the shoes of the head of science in a pharmaceutical company when they are having a disagreement about how to position a drug if they have a pre-existing relationship. Thinking about it, this seems logical. How many times though do we try to skip that relationship-building stage? Do we ask people to just jump into the other person's shoes? Research suggests this could be a false economy.

We can also hypothesize about context. In a big room full of people who all work together, the small group you work with every day would likely be first in line for your empathy. If you were at a networking event with a colleague that you'd not met before but you know still works for the same organization, along with a range of people from other organizations who you've never met, that colleague would probably qualify for your empathy.

There are many different ways to create external environments that nudge people towards connecting.

NEIL MORRISON - HR DIRECTOR, RANDOM HOUSE GROUP

We took the entire London organization to Brighton for a conference and we had a gala dinner at which everyone sat down dining together. The impact of that on people, looking down from this balcony at all these tables and chairs and understanding the size but then spending the evening together, sitting with people, talking with people. We did a similar piece with the Christmas party. Now a lot of people would have said that the organization is too big to do this now, we can't do this, but I think the importance of doing that and just realizing the value of breaking bread together, effectively, it comes back to human-to-human interaction. When you do that, people form those bonds and then you bump into a person in the corridor that you were on the dance floor with and that has been really important. We had to probably engineer it a bit more over the last year than they would have done because we are trying to put those two organizations together, but thereafter I think it's about allowing people to do it organically and that is how it works best, in my view. Valuing connection, so stating as an organization it's important, and allowing people the time to do it, is great. Then you find that they kind of contacted each other and start thinking, "Would he do something similar to me? We should probably talk," that gets things done much more quickly and efficiently then the leadership trying to do it.

Neil recognizes that you can't *make* people connect. Their internal environment (their brain and mind) is a big factor. However, you can invest in creating opportunities that will serve individuals and the organization going forward. You can also hear trust coming through in this organization, that once people are given the opportunity and the time to do what will benefit them and the company, they are doing it.

These opportunities don't have to all be big. Encouraging individuals to reach out to others in small ways can offer the same benefits. People often know how they like to connect with others, whether they prefer a big event or to suggest to their desk neighbor they go for a walk at lunch. We just need organizations and cultures that value connecting. This extends to clients. In many professions where the personal connection has been squeezed out through policies, time pressures, and targets, engagement and performance has dropped while absence has increased.

We just need organizations and cultures that value connecting

Positive Empathy

Recent advances have enabled us to distinguish positive empathy from general positivity and empathy for people in distress.[10] Positive empathy correlates with positive things such as prosocial behavior, social closeness, and wellbeing. In Buddhism, finding joy in others' happiness and success is one of the four central virtues.[11] We know that positive emotion promotes social bonding, making it easier for us to openly connect and engage with others.[12] A neuroimaging study showed that people could experience rewards for someone they're close to as strongly as if the reward was for themselves.[13] It is worth noting that when people are under cognitive load (a frequent occurrence in many workplaces) positive empathy can be dampened.[14] The excitement that positive empathy is related to social connection including closeness, trust and relationship satisfaction, prosocial behavior including emotional support and tangible assistance, and wellbeing including life satisfaction, is great. It means that cultivating positive empathy is a good thing to do.

What Does This Mean Practically?

Consider how well things are set up in your organization to help people develop their empathetic joy. Do you share the positive things that have happened at the start of meetings? Do people genuinely feel happy for other's success? Is there a way for different departments to hear about the good things happening in one another's working life? Remember with all of these things to make it as personal as possible. Understanding what an achievement means to someone is far more powerful than just hearing that the achievement has been made.

Differences between People

We are often asked when we are working with organizations whether different people have different types of brains (or words to a similar effect). We know experientially that people respond differently to the same situation. This different behavior could be linked to slight differences in the wiring of the brain, genes, neurotransmitters, or a range of other variables.

For example, recently the first evidence that our childhood experiences of paternal warmth moderates the effect of vasopressin on empathic concern has been uncovered.[15] In people who reported higher levels of paternal warmth, vasopressin increased the empathetic concern people showed when watching distressing or uplifting videos. It is possible that a father's parenting style may effect epigenetic modification of vasopressin receptors.

Men and women are affected differently in terms of their accurate perception of social interactions when a boost of oxytocin is administered. In one study, participants were shown various video clips of social interactions. They were asked to answer questions that focused on identifying relationships of kinship, intimacy, and competition. In general, everyone improved in their ability to interpret social interactions after having the oxytocin. However there was a difference between men and women, which fits with other research. Men's ability to correctly interpret competitive relationships improved and women's ability to identify kinship improved.

What Does This NOT Mean?

This type of research does not mean that people with cold fathers can't be empathetic. That is an example of taking one piece of research in isolation and running with it to a point of untruth. We know the brain is very complex and multiple factors often feed into outputs. We also know it is very plastic. We also wouldn't want to summarize that women *can't* identify competitive relationships or that men *can't* identify relationships of kin.[16]

JANE OLDS – HEAD OF HR, WEATHERBYS

Our culture is quite unusual; it was for me when I arrived because I came from a corporate environment. You walk in to this business and from day one via the induction we are encouraging people to be open and friendly in the corridors to everybody and then we try to encourage that informal relaxed environment. It's something that both the Weatherbys encourage; they walk around the business and talk and smile to people when they see them. As a part of the induction program we introduce everybody to them. So what we have very much hopefully is that people would join, find that other people they know would talk to them and say Hi, and I think that in itself then, people tend to follow it and so they need to lead by example and do the same. I'd like to think that people feel that the culture here is very warm and friendly. We do have evidence of it because we do four weeks reviews, three months reviews, and one of our questions is, How are you finding our culture and how are you finding the work within your area? and it's always positive and hopefully that reflects the culture is as that we would like to portray, certainly from the Weatherbys' perspective, just what they want to continue as we grow. It's tough to grow, I have to say; the more people are in the business, the harder it is to maintain that informality – but we've been able to maintain it up to now.

Communicating the Connection

So let's imagine that you've loved this chapter. You have bought into the reassuring truth that connection offers a lot to your organization. There is just one potential challenge, you're not sure that everyone else feels the same ... yet. A common challenge. Let's look at what some of the neuroscience research has uncovered that could help us.

One study involved scanning people when they first received an idea that was later going to be their responsibility to spread. It was found that the ideas that were later spread successfully had a couple of components in common.[17] Normally the idea was valued by the receiver. This may have been because they connected with the idea themselves or they could image others doing so. This may involve brain regions involved in reward and positive evaluations, such as the ventral striatum and ventromedial prefrontal cortex. The second component requires the individual to accurately predict the person's interests and preferences that they're sharing the idea with. This process typically recruits the dorsomedial prefrontal cortex (DMPFC) and the temporoparietal junction. These areas are thought to be involved in successful communication during a narrative.[18]

Imagine the positive impact ideas that could spread with a buzz would have. Imagine the idea being received by your colleague's brain in a way that they want to share it with others. There are a couple of processes that can additionally contribute to an idea creating a buzz. One is the idea salesperson effect, which you read about earlier in this chapter. The other is the intention effect, which involves the medial prefrontal cortex and precuneus/posterior cingulate cortex, associated with self-relevance processing. Overall the buzz effect involves regions of the brain important for reward processing (that is the ventral striatum) and mentalizing (TPJ and DMPFC).[17]

Again a core message here is to align your strategy with the activities you are doing. Partner with an organization, like Synaptic Potential, who have both a broad understanding of what is important to get results and also the specific deeper insights into the ways to do it. Engaging people is both an art and a science. We now have various checklists to assess where organizations are at and the state specific initiatives are in. Putting the science behind endeavors doesn't guarantee success – the brain is complex – the brains of many add another level of complexity – but it does make success more likely.

Engaging people is both an art and a science

Getting Things Done

In organizations we work with we often hear from people that it can be tricky to get things done. To get a new initiative accepted and engaged with can be a challenge. Here is where the reassuring truth can be really useful. Ideally you want the infrastructure in place well before you need to draw upon it.

DAVID JAMES – FORMER L&D, DISNEY, FOUNDER OF WECOMMEND.COM

So what we would do is, again it is so tactical. I must say that I wasn't at all political before I got in to Disney, but I think I got the hang of it really quickly, so I'll let you in on what I did. When I first joined I was an advisor acting as a manager, and there were some strong HR manager characters. So when I went to launch or prelaunch the program, I identified the three most influential and I went to them on a one-to-one and said,

"Look I'm thinking of launching this, in your experience, what worked, what didn't work?" So what you do is meet with them all one-to-one, and then when you are in the meeting you say, "So if I did this, would you back me in front of the other HR managers?" So three made ones who are alongside you and then you go to all the others all in one meeting and go, "Look we are launching this here, at the benefit of speaking with person X, person Y, person Z, I'd love for you to share your thoughts," everyone said, "I think it's a brilliant idea and I think we all should get behind it, it's important for our business." So I'd then just chip in, "OK, so we've produced these documents, if you would like to take them away let us know how you would like this tailored for your business." So you can see, it's a very tactical approach to get one thing done. Now the only thing that really changed was how it was presented to the business, the rest of it wasn't personalized at all, it was a one standard approach, but it was one that it was built with key stakeholders within it.

This was about getting things done. If I was absolutely sure that what I knew the organization needed was a mentoring program then I'd find a way of getting that done, and I'd have to stake my reputation on that being the right solution to get that done and bring people with me. That is just how things get done and that is the way I saw it. . . .

What's the Bottom Line?

Social connection is incredibly powerful.
Treat people as real people.

What Can I Do Today?

Meet someone for a coffee with the pure intention of getting to know them better, of reaching out and connecting with another human more deeply.

What Can I Put in Place for the Long Term?

Work on creating a culture where connection is valued. Trust people to trust themselves. Make it easy through your strategies, systems, policies, and management pieces for people to connect both internally and externally.

What Is the Overall Ideal Vision?

The vision is an organization where people value, respect, and deeply connect with each other. The ideal is that people love spending time with their colleagues; they are good friends.

part III

How Do We Motivate People?

This is the question people most often ask, however we need to flip it around. We need to be asking, how do we stop de-motivating people? Addressing the question at an individual level won't get the biggest results. This section is about the practices and the culture that will support people in being themselves and doing what they're good at.

Frederic Laloux introduces[1] a compelling case for a new way of being and doing for organizations. He suggests that the Pluralistic-Green perspective, distinct from the Conformist-Amber, Achievement-Orange or Impulsive-Red ones, is uneasy with power and hierarchy. This whole part of the book echo's the sentiments of an Evolutionary-Teal organization and gives some scientific underpinning as to why it would make sense to move forward. Some of the ideas are pretty out-there. They will make many CEOs feel uncomfortable. They will also make many employees feel uncomfortable. Why? Our brains have adapted to what the norm is now.

> There is nothing inherently "better" about being at a higher level of development, just as an adolescent is not "better" than a toddler. However, the fact remains that an adolescent is able to do more, because he or she can think in more sophisticated ways than a toddler.

Any level of development is okay; the question is whether that level of development is a good fit for the task at hand.

(Nick Petrie)

So we've pulled together an internal comms toolkit, so that if you have some organizational change initiative or something that you think you need to communicate, you can use that as a form of doing it. On the issue of how we celebrate, we recently underwent a review of our salary and grading structure and as part of that we received feedback commenting on how stingy the pay benefits and salary are, we need to be making up for it on some other non-financial benefits. We responded and recently ran a benefits fair, where we had people from all our benefits providers, whether that is child care, give the people our back to work scheme, the employee helpline, pensions, just to try to enable people to learn factually but within a full environment: "I didn't realize that," "I didn't know I was eligible for a sabbatical," that kind of thing. [...] Another thing that we've done to try to get people to be engaged in and involved, we recently launched something that is in recognition of the fact that not everybody in the business here gets a chance to travel overseas. There are business units where they need to go and visit programs but some do not, most of the HR don't. So we've got a scheme whereby each year we are selecting or choosing, scoring, four entries, the winners will get the opportunity to go and visit a lot of programs overseas. It creates a "wow factor," because people can see that long-serving employees have been rewarded in that particular way both inside and outside, but also what that does is allows a transfer of learning from us to the countries we've visited, and we could then bring it back.

Within my team, I've spent quite a bit of time deliberately to try to get them to feel value within ActionAid. They are recognized within the third sector but also it disturbs me that within the HR community as a whole I think that people sometimes think that all the good people are in the private and not the charity sector. I have got some superb people in my team but unless you get recognition for that you are going to end up disengaged so we were happy to recently be featured in the HR magazine.

ANGELA O'CONNOR — HR LOUNGE

How would I actually describe HR? I've always thought of it as the engine room that drives the business whatever that business is, public or private it really doesn't matter. For me, the only differentiator we have in organizations is people; I've always seen our job as being able to release the potential in individuals, so to help people find the best that they can do themselves, also working with managers to really sort out the things that they woke up in the night worrying about and most managers worry most about people issues more than anything else when you start to unravel it. So I've always seen our job as really being able to fire up that engine room of the organization and create success through the people initiatives.

Will this be the future of HR? Or might the picture be quite different?

chapter 7

The Synaptic Circle

We are often constrained by our brains. We may think about what is possible through the lens of what we've seen previously. These two chapters do the same, giving you safe, comfortable small stretches while hopefully also tempting you to think bigger. Consider the opportunities to rewrite how things could be. If you want people to be genuinely motivated then small changes may not be enough. You may be trying to fit a round peg into a square hole.

Control

Neuroscience of Control

It is believed that we have capacity for voluntary control over our actions.[1] Factors that influence a person's sense of control are considered big deals. Prisons and psychosis have a big effect on people. Although Libet's early work on the neuroscience of free will is very important,[2] here we will chunk up a little and focus in on the practical level.

In a now well-publicized study, researchers set out to see whether there was a difference in effect when people self-administered or yoked cocaine injections. Essentially, the participants first self-administered the drug and then later they were given the same amount but didn't have control over the administration. The results were quite powerful. During yoked experiments the cardiovascular safety parameters were exceeded, meaning the volunteers bodies' responded differently.[3] Another experiment that also looked at the effects of self-administering versus another having control with cocaine also showed that it can affect the response.[4]

When we look there have been lots of experiments that showed this same pattern including electric shocks, morphine and midazolam.

We don't know exactly what is happening in every situation where a person's control is taken away from them, however it is fair to suspect a threat response is generated on many occasions.

Ideas

Control is really important for people to have. You can be creative in how people are given control over things within the organization. Some organizations are embracing some innovative ways forward on this, some are using old-school, comfortable ideas from this list, some are experimenting with new ideas, which may make you feel uneasy! Consider the employees:

be creative in how people are given control

- Being responsible for creating a CSR initiative and running it
- Leading committees, such as a social committee responsible for putting on social events throughout the year
- Being enabled to set their own goals/targets/objectives
- Exploring new products or services to offer
- Being responsible for setting and managing their own budgets
- Contributing to the values
- Choosing how, where or when they work
- Taking as much holiday as they want
- Choosing their bosses
- Not having bosses! – Peer relationships without hierarchy

Practical Examples

I asked several leaders how they give people control within the organization. Here are some responses.

NEIL MORRISON - HR DIRECTOR, RANDOM HOUSE GROUP

That is a really interesting question! I think that over-engineered organizations create an environment where people don't think that they can take control or they are scared to take control because they worry about the consequences. We wanted to manage and design this new organization to foster adult relationships, which is "We will trust you and you will take responsibility and that is the deal." You can't ask to be trusted but not take responsibility, and we can't ask you to take responsibility unless we trust you. In terms of where we are going through change, there is quite a lot of courage required from people to do that, because it's often safer to not take control. It's not as engaging and it's not as enjoyable perhaps but it's sometime safer to say, "I was just following orders, it wasn't me." So I think it requires quite a strong leadership message that it's okay; it requires a culture that says that you won't be blamed when things go wrong, because things *will* go wrong, we know it. In particular, when you are merging two companies, lots of stuff goes wrong, every day. We've got to get used to that, be okay with that.

I don't think you can create an environment where people take control overnight. I think it's a lot of reinforcements over a period of time. It like the total quality management, the approach of the Japanese car makers: if you see a problem, you take action with the problem, you don't go, "Well, that wasn't my bit." Ultimately it's about being focused on successful output rather than it is my input only in this bit.

I wouldn't say as an organization we are 100 percent great. I would say we are better than a lot of organizations, but I think we've got a lot further to go to be a truly empowered organization, and some of that is just practice, habit, and rein-forcements. [...] I think it comes through often role-modelling behaviors from senior level, people to see that actually if you do take control and there are repercussions if things go wrong, it's okay. Also it's about all your people management practices actually reinforcing that, because if you say one thing but ulti-mately your organization is designed in another way, to take away control, then it's not a coherent message. For example, we've just done a piece around internal mobility and we've been saying to people, you are responsible for your careers, you ultimately own those decisions, but our responsibility is to cre-ate an environment where you are free to own that and could do that without fear of retribution, so if you go and explore an opportunity somewhere else in the organization, you are not going to kill your career opportunities in the part of the organization that you are in. Our job is to create environments through the culture and the practices, and just to reinforce the message with people.

JABBAR SADDAR – DIRECTOR OF HR & OD, CAFCASS

If you give them more power, autonomy, in terms of how to do the job but how to then support themselves when they actually need that support followed up by internal HR, you get really good motivation. This is the third time we've rebalanced the approach in that way, because historically most organizations hold up power in terms of what they do with their staff, when they do it, or what they are offering. What we wanted to do is to say to our staff, you've done your job and we want you to actu-ally have a say in this, and they voted for it. We asked the staff, "If we brought this in, would you use it? If we brought it in, what are the other six or seven important elements of the health and wellbeing plan?" ... The majority of our staff said that they would use it and this is a good idea, and we've got 99 percent take-up of the health and wellbeing plan within the organization.

(The 1 percent that don't take it is because they already have an equivalent plan that includes their partners, having two plans doesn't really work.) So, it's almost 100 per cent uptake, and that is my proudest achievement because that has helped increase engagement and to improve the quality of work and reduce sickness. Within our organization, with social work staff, our sickness rate is not the lowest but amongst the lowest in the whole of the public sector.

Might future organizations eliminate targets that assume we can predict the future, that take our attention away from inner motivation and trusting our instincts and narrow our focus so we miss new opportunities?

Consider many of the prevalent behaviors that are linked to targets. Spending a year's remaining budget, just so it doesn't go down next year. Not continuing to push forward in sales once targets are met, so it doesn't go up next year. Huge chunks of time spent trying to agree targets in the first place, only for all parties to not be fully happy.

Celebration

Neuroscience of Celebration

When we talk about celebrating, we're talking about activating the reward networks in the brain: triggering a dopamine boost, a serotonin boost, even a release of oxytocin. Making people feel good is the aim. Celebration is an opportunity to decrease levels of cortisol. It helps shape our brain to make it easier to be positive, happy, and even joyful tomorrow.

Ideas

What can you celebrate? Absolutely anything you choose. You may like to focus in on whatever it is that you know is congruent with your organization. What contribution are you making? How do people feed into that? What you celebrate and don't celebrate shapes people's brains. By giving people autonomy around how and when they celebrate, you set things up to be more powerful. While big parties are great and important, you also want the spontaneous opportunities to be utilized.

• Recognition – public and one-to-one
• Freedom for teams to choose when and how they celebrate
• Going out for a team lunch
• Taking a whole day off after a big project to go on an outdoor adventure
• Playing a game
• Starting meetings by sharing something positive
• One day a year reach out to people you serve and thank them for working with you

Practical Examples

NEIL MORRISON – HR DIRECTOR, RANDOM HOUSE GROUP

At all of our board meetings the first thing we do is talk about trophy moments, where they want to share and celebrate. Some of it will be personal and some of it will be professional. So it could be, "actually last weekend I went out and threw myself out of an airplane; I've never done that before and for me – I'm scared of heights – that was a great moment for me." Or it could be, "I'm just through the restructure of my team; it's gone really successfully, people are genuinely understanding and I'm really proud of that." So, that is on a micro-level.

We have quarterly briefings where we would also celebrate success for all employees, or it could be a named individual, so with the CEO we would talk about, 'actually it would be really great if you could just give a bit of recognition to this person, because they've been doing this...' The receptionist, for example, might be the payroll manager, it won't necessarily always be the rain-makers, they get enough celebration as it is, but again, it's very individual, it's very personal, rather then it being formal recognition schemes or anything like, 'Well you haven't had it last year so we need to give you a badge this month' sort of approach.

It does tend to be very personalized and we encourage leaders to celebrate within their areas and to recognize that different people like different types of recognition. So understand what they really value. It could be actually, 'Can you go and pick up the kids from school? Off you go, because I know that's really important, you've been working late and you haven't had the chance to do it so I want you to go and do it," or someone else might be able to leave and spend the weekend in a spa. It's a real kind of celebrating achievements and recognizing it but individually rather than through something formal.

I think the other thing is for the organization now and we are talking a lot about the success of this organization, which comes back to this. There are difficult messages and actually talking about what you have achieved is really important, because otherwise people just focus on the bad stuff. [...] The only other thing we are focused on is it's got to be genuine celebration, because actually, celebrating stuff that isn't really worth celebrating just loses the effect. You are better off not doing it than you are over emphasizing it.

LOUISA FRYER – CATH KIDSON

How would we say we celebrate? I think that we could probably do a bit around that, I think that we are not as active on that at the moment. People *are* recognized but it is not in a big-bang way, it's quite informal. We have an annual event that happens either between Christmas and summer. So we've got partners that come over on Christmas, so it's too much pressure on business to do all that then, so we'll have our big celebration around then and there is usually lots of fun, and there is a competition for the best-dressed team. The last year we had Halloween, there were lots of skeletons. That was fun and the design team won that; they were all dressed up like horror outfits. It was really good.

Might the future organization feel like a positive place to work? Where people genuinely celebrate one another's achievements and live from a place of gratitude rather than fear?

Confidence

Neuroscience of Confidence

When we think of self-confidence as something involving the brain circuitry of self-doubt and anxiety, we can gain some valuable insights. The synaptic connections in our brain shape us and ultimately lead to the expression of who we are.[5] Further research is likely to help us more fully understand our subjective experience of confidence. However we do know that being in a state of confidence is linked to the chemicals we release and subsequently our behavior, so it is important to consider. We want people spending most of their time confident in what they are doing, and feeling safe when they stretch themselves.

Ideas

- Enable people to identify the areas they need to grow in and then do so through accessing resources (people, training, coaching, books).
- Give people time to develop.
- Encourage people to safely try new things and stretch themselves.
- Invite people to shape their roles.
- Share information with people.
- Organize things so people can access what they need.

Practical Examples

Social media app company Buffer gives employees and family members a kindle with unlimited books. At the French brass foundry FAVI, self-management principles are prevalent. The typical hierarchical structure was deconstructed and teams set up instead. They self-organize with no middle management instructing them. There is no HR, planning, scheduling, engineering, production-IT, or purchasing departments. Each team takes responsibility for what needs to be done and they are confident in their abilities. They haven't had a late delivery in over 25 years. This different way of working and structuring the whole organization means that they have far greater confidence in what needs to be done and how to do it, and even whether they can do it.

Certainty

Neuroscience of Certainty

Our brain seeks out patterns to recognize. It wants to predict what is going to happen next. This helps keep us safe. If something is different to what we expect then we pay attention.[6] When there is uncertainty, an error response is generated in the orbital frontal cortex. This can happen when there is incongruency, for example, between what a leader says and does. Experientially we know that in times of great uncertainty (job security, role expectations, promotion criteria) our performance is impacted. The neuroscience of attention would suggest that uncertainty draws our attention, and with a limited supply this means it is taken away from something else.[7]

It is not the case that people always need certainty. The power of uncertainty can be harnessed at appropriate times and in productive ways, for example to draw attention. Frequently though, in organizations the lack of certainty leads to the threat response and prolonged elevated cortisol levels.

Ideas

We have lots of opportunities within an organization to offer certainty to our people.

• Communicate, even when there is nothing new to say.
• Be honest, trustworthy, and reliable.

- Involve people to the degree that they are creating their own certainty.
- Enable people to write their own job descriptions with a level of detail they have clarity with.
- Facilitate connection with the core contribution people are making, while circumstances may change, that they can be certain of.

Practical Examples

ANDREA CARTRIGHT, HR DIRECTOR, SUPERGROUP

We hire a lot of young people into stores week in and week out. When I first came in, a manager would give you a job, you can start on Monday and if you were lucky, we'd remember to put you on payroll. If you were even more lucky, you might get a contract of employment about six months after you've arrived, by which time most people have already left. And that contract for employment would say you were working for a company called "Cult Retail Ltd," which is one of our group companies and it is the banner under which our retail business trades, but of course for you, you think, "I thought I came to work for SuperDry, there is no mention of SuperDry anywhere." [This is] the stuff that we completely reversed out; we do get people on the payroll within 24 hours of offering them a job, and they get a lovely little starter guide. It could be better, but it is a starter guide. It's about how SuperDry came to be, what is so fantastic about, what we expect you to wear to work – it's not a list of you can't do this and you can't do that – it's, you know, we want you to look amazing every day, we want you to be showcasing our products. It's all kind of really positive stuff. And a letter that says this is your contract, and it's written in English, rather than, "Thou shall not do this, don't do this..."

What's the Bottom Line?

You want to think about how people have control, celebrate, are confident, and get certainty.

What Can I Do Today?

Share your thoughts with a colleague. By now you will have some instincts around where the organization's strengths and opportunities lie, so reach out to someone and discuss your ideas with them.

What Can I Put in Place for the Long Term?

The opportunity is to revolutionize how things are organized. A lynchpin is likely to be for the organization to give up control. To hand back control to the individuals who choose to come and work with the organization. So the bigger piece is to consider who would need to start exploring these ideas to make some big changes.

What Is the Overall Ideal Vision?

The vision is an organization where people are valued and enabled to be human. The organization is seen as an entity that people work with. There is a healthy, positive feel and level of respect present.

8

Are You Capitalizing on a Neuro-friendly Culture?

Your culture is incredibly powerful. It is similar to a human's character. Future companies will have strong cultures that are authentic. Throughout this book a common theme is congruency. Things need to line up so expectations are clean and clear. Having a culture riddled with incongruences is a big problem. Many organizations invest time and money into creating shared values. These are then on the walls, on the website, and in various documents. The problem is that they are not real values. What really is valued is other things.

What neuroscience is pointing to is similar to some ideas from the area of servant leadership. Robert K. Greenleaf first wrote about 'The Servant as Leader', in an essay published in 1970. [1]

> The difference manifests itself in the care taken by the servant-first to make sure that other people's highest priority needs are being served. The best test, and difficult to administer, is: Do those served grow as persons? Do they, while being served, become healthier, wiser, freer, more autonomous, more likely themselves to become servants? And, what is the effect on the least privileged in society? Will they benefit or at least not be further deprived?

This thinking was followed up by the idea that organizations could be servant-leaders too.[1]

Whereas, until recently, caring was largely person to person, now most of it is mediated through institutions – often large, complex, powerful, impersonal; not always competent; sometimes corrupt. If a better society is to be built, one that is more just and more loving, one that provides greater creative opportunity for its people, then the most open course is to raise both the capacity to serve and the very performance as servant of existing major institutions by new regenerative forces operating within them.

Many of the points that are raised when we consider these areas have previously been considered soft or fluffy. Maybe because previously there wasn't the scientific understanding of what happened to people in the presence or absence of them? We now have a body of evidence from observing organizations and our scientific body of evidence. The next stage would be to couple these up more experimentally.

Your Metaphor

What is your metaphor? When new people join your organization, how do they know what the culture is like? Many organizations talk about being part of a family, being in it together, looking after each other and helping each other out. Southwest Airlines suggest people display "a servant's heart" and "embrace the SWA family."

A new group of organizations that have emerged independently from one another share a common metaphor. They often talk about their organizations as a living organism or living system. This reflects the wisdom, complexity, wholeness, and change that are key qualities of this new type of place to be.

Trust

Neuroscience of Trust

Why is trust so important? Evolutionarily it makes sense that we are wired for trust. In human's history it was likely that if you were untrustworthy or you didn't have people around you whom you could trust, then you might die. Most people would say they prefer to be around people they can trust, that it is a quality we still value in others. Many organizations say they think it is important and they want to be trusted by employees and clients.

What do we know about trust?[2]

- More oxytocin is linked to behaving in a more trustworthy way.
- If you feel trusted, you release more oxytocin becoming more trustworthy.
- Demonstrating trustworthiness activates ventral tegmental areas – the brain's reward centers.
- Trust reduces the amygdala's activity levels.
- Threat and fear responses are lowered.
- If trust is breached, the anterior cingulate cortex detects conflict and activates the amygdala.
- High stress blocks the release of oxytocin.
- When men feel distrusted, a rise in dihydrotestosterone has been seen. This increases the desire for physical confrontation.

Ideas

Check out the easy to remember TRUST approach:
- **Truth** – speak it, not a version of it, not leaving bits out, the whole truth and nothing but the truth.
- **Reliability** – do what you say you will
- **Understand** – seek to really understand what is being expected of you; make yourself understood in terms of what you are asking of others.
- **Show** – others you trust them. Be prepared to practice forgiveness; it is a skill.
- **Transparency** – are you happy with everyone knowing this? If not, is the reason to benefit you above others?

Here are some additional ideas at work in the organization FAVI:

- Trust teams with the overall reality. For FAVI that is the fact that competition from China is stiff. The level of ownership teams have is motivational. Work becomes an adventure not a bind.

- The teams decide budgets for projects. They don't haggle with the boss and so don't come in with inflated numbers; they are honest about their needs.
- The "ideas scout," who travels the world looking for good ideas, proves his worth to the teams. He is trusted to be reasonable with travel and hotel expenses.
- Once the clocking-in system was abolished, productivity increased. This was because people could work at their natural optimum rate, rather than slowing themselves down so targets didn't get raised too high. They also now sometimes choose to stay late to finish a job they take pride in.

BEN BENGOUGAM – VICE PRESIDENT HUMAN RESOURCES, EMEA, HILTON WORLDWIDE

I certainly think trust is important. We measure it as part of our yearly survey. We measure trust and we measure engagement and obviously trust and engagement correlate. These are pretty universal, not culture specific in a sense. How people feel about the organization, how people feel about Hilton universally in every country.

We major on trust and major on engagement. We believe they are universal concepts. These are part of our values and our vision and mission. We believe we achieve them through our people and that's pretty universal. How that has manifested itself varies. Some countries are concerned with the basic stuff. I've just come back from South Africa recently and people working in the hotels in Johannesburg about a mile from the township, so most employees live in the township. These people live in a rather underprivileged environment and yet work in an opulent environment. When I think about them and when I think about what we deliver to them, a lot of it is around the basic stuff. We have to provide them with safety and security.

> In some cases we have to provide them with the only meal they have every day.
>
> As people go up the career ladder, their motivations become more sophisticated. The notion of getting to the hearts and minds of people to drive performance is important to us.
>
> We conduct a survey every year, we take it very seriously. 150,000 people from around the world are invited to complete it and 92 percent of people do. We get over 80 percent engagement, close to 90 percent on trust. We publish the results, we action plan, we incentivize leadership behaviors to ensure we not only talk about the right culture but we espouse it and we behave it. We lead by example. We take it very seriously.

One HR director shared this next piece, which I think really shows how far some organizations have got to travel.

> If we want this we've got to do the hard work [...] We could all put up on pieces of paper and go, "These are the things that we want to do," but actually the hard work is really us living it and making sure that we are willing to change the way in which we operate to reinforce that. So often it's easy to say, 'Oh yes, we want to be transparent,' and he would say, 'OK, are we willing to be transparent about pay?' Oh no. So we don't want to be transparent, do we? We can't say we want to trust people. It's all those telltale [signs] that ultimately counteract what we say. We say one thing and then we behave in another way and wonder why people don't recognize what we are saying.

Fairness

A culture of fairness is refreshing. It is also, unsurprisingly, affects how we feel about our work. For example, people who are paid less than their peers rate their job satisfaction less favorably.[3] We know that fairness and cooperation are rewarding. When we see fairness, our reward centers light up. The ventral striatum, amygdala and orbitofrontal cortex, and ventromedial prefrontal cortex are activated with this intuitive reaction. Conversely, the insula lights up when we believe something to be unfair. In the "ultimatum" game, the more the anterior insula lit up, the more likely a person was to reject the offer.[4] The anterior cingulate cortex is involved in evaluating whether an outcome is met or is different from our expectations. It is also involved when we suffer social losses, such as being treated unfairly.

Connection

We looked at the neuroscience of connection in Chapter 6. The opportunity in organizations that want to honor the human nature of their people is to encourage a culture where connection is valued. The power of this is great. A person who feels that they are part of a family, that they have friends as well as colleagues, that they can look out for others and will be looked out for also is a secure person.

LUCY SENTENCE – HR BUSINESS PARTNER, MATHWORKS

I think we have a huge culture of investment in our people, I've never personally worked or know of anybody who has worked anywhere that has ... as an organization really committed to investing in the training and genuine development of the employees, literally from day one when the on-boarding starts. There is a huge investment from many, many people. There is a lot of work structure that has gone in to having plans as a minimum to every new employee, that gives you a really broad view and understanding of how the organization works, what's important here at Mathworks, a value-driven organization. Everyone goes over to our headquarters in Boston for a couple of weeks, and up to two months, to attend what is called the big picture orientation and that is one of the most valuable and certainly engaging parts of that round part plan. You really see how much people are investing in you, all the way up to the CEO who spends time every month with all of the new hires in the company, I don't know anywhere else that that happens. Further to that, there is obviously dedicated training hours and managers are very carefully selected and developed in order to work most effectively. I think that has been, in my view, the biggest surprise and one of the biggest benefits of coming here – to see the investment in everyone and the opportunities for your own development that takes place.

In some organizations people are geographically spread out. This can cause some concerns.

LUCY SENTENCE – HR BUSINESS PARTNER, MATHWORKS

There are lots of scheduled meetings based on different managers and their employees will have one-on-one on a regular basis, usually every one or two weeks, there are multiple team meetings and there is lots of processing to make sure that when we are making decisions, for example recruiting decisions, that there are meetings to set up a recruitment team so everybody is aligned in what they are looking for in the new hire, for example, and then we wrap up again at the end so that everybody shares their information. [...] That is an example of how [we] support that collaboration and interaction. Then another development side of this is that [...] you have to be prepared for other people to get in to your work, asking questions and challenging you; that is very much part of the culture, so that helps ensure that you're not drifting away or losing contact and becoming isolated in your own location.

I think investment in getting people over for the big meetings, every year there is a company kick-off meeting and everybody is brought together globally. There is a very strategic view to making sure when there is a lot of value to be gained from meeting face-to-face there is opportunity to take it. So if you get that chance to build a relationship with people and that makes it possible for you to use the technology very effectively to maintain that relationship and keep the contacts. There is definitely a recognition that in terms of building early relationships and really making sure people align you can't really get the same value anywhere as you can from a face-to-face interaction, so there is a foundation there and then we build on them.

A: Can you tell us more about the kick-off meeting? What kind of structure or things go on in there in order to make the most of that face-to-face opportunity?

L: There will be a social element to it; there will also be a kind of retrospective, you know, what happened in the last 12 months, how has the company been performing, what was your part in that; and there will be a kind of success story shared and people will look and recognize the team, the people. There is also a forward planning aspect in that you look at making a strategy for the year ahead, basically setting things up to be able to work more effectively throughout the year while you are not in one place. There is a lot of focus on team building and that sort of social element and making sure that people get benefit of working with all these likeminded individuals that enjoy our time together as well.

JO DEADMAN – HEAD OF TALENT, BRITISH GAS

How will we change habits?

It's like dieting. If you tell me I need to eat less for the rest of my life, it isn't going to happen. If you tell me I can't have chocolate, it isn't going to happen. But there are things that we can encourage you to do rather than not do. So where talent is concerned with habits, we want to try to engage with more collaboration.

We want to make things easy for people to participate in.

How do we facilitate connection?

I'm seeing a lot of touch points in the development route.

There is genuine respect for others within the business. I don't think that comes from any particular experience, I see it coming from a genuine interest people have in each other and therefore their professional ability to do their job well.

If you'd told me 18 months ago I'd be working for a utilities company I'd have said, "yeah, yeah." It took me a while to get under the skin of the business, but meeting the individuals I did meet through the interview process absolutely nailed it for me. I think you can be attracted to an organization by the people.

Reward Networks

Remember that a big part of motivation is about activating the reward networks. Midbrain dopamine neurons appear to signal a reward prediction error, enabling us to predict and act to increase the probability of a reward in the future.[5] A culture that is free to enable individuals to activate reward networks should be a motivated culture.

a big part of motivation is about activating the reward networks

GRAHAM SALISBURY – HEAD OF HR, ACTIONAID UK

We are the second best performing HR team in the country, but does it mean that the people would feel good about what they are doing if they got some external recognition? Yes. Does it motivate them? Yes! Does it make the rest of the building, the people here feel good? Yes, it does. Therefore I think going for that external recognition is something, to create that feel good factor. Also what happens as a result of that, it spins off of people, almost like this: "You did that, can you help us?" And that brings to a couple of other things that we've been doing, where we are trying as hard as we can to share almost anything and everything that we do. There was an article in *People* magazine in November about this ... my HR team, because what we did was – the back end of last year – we delivered, through an external person, a three-day module on improving HR business.

NEIL MORRISON – HR DIRECTOR, RANDOM HOUSE GROUP

We're in a strange place because we merged a year ago. A lot of our work is around how do you bring people together in a time when there is quite a lot of change and perceived challenge and fear. I think in the last year we've been able to manage and navigate through that very well. There have been difficult decisions and changes but they have always been communicated incredibly well and we've been able to deliver them without creating more trauma than we need to. At the same time, we've been dismantling two organizations and building another and that is the excitement and balancing those two things has been really exciting and interesting.[...]

A lot of it is telling people bad stuff, being open about it, so they know that if there is a bad message, that you will be telling them. Trust and transparency are really critical to this, and so for example, we had to do some work bringing together our benefits portfolio, and we went out and we said, "This is the problem," to all employees. "You lot get this, you lot get that, we can't afford to give all of you this," and just being very open and honest and very clear around the challenges. They may not like it but they do understand it. It's that, "I don't like it but I understand you've got to find some solution." It's been about focusing on positives as well as some of the challenges. At the same time, so there are very additional ways of bringing two organizations together, or there are some very exciting ways of doing it and I think we've been very mindful of asking, "is there an exciting way we can do this?" each time, because actually it is not about hiding the bad stuff, but if you say, "actually this is quite painful, but look at the end of it, we've got to this and this is a lot better" which helps people transition a lot better.

I think that the open honest conversations, and the communication to everyone, it isn't a bunch of people going off behind closed doors but being open and accessible, over indexing on senior people being available, talking to people, communicating with people. So that there is also that opportunity to ask questions has been fundamental.

[...]For example, we've set up so the CEO has breakfast with all new joiners, as a group not individually otherwise he'd be having breakfast all the time. Once a month he has a lunch with a random group of employees from across the organizations. We have set up a staff forum so we have an opportunity to interface with him and with me. With any change piece, for example with the benefit piece, I went and visited every single site, we did presentations all day so people could come and ask questions and talk to you so it is a real human-to human piece, rather than organization-to-pleb piece and I think that has been really important. We are an organization who is very human because the people who work here are all about publishing and books and passion.

Neil and the team at Random House Group are being mindful of:

Trust

Certainty

Connection

Fairness

They are demonstrating that consistent investment into the relationships within the organizations is worth it to them. This is wise because organizations often make demands on people when times are tough, but haven't got the connection between employee and company to sustain this. Changing someone's benefits is a tricky endeavor. People could feel that things are uncertain, they can't trust the company, and that things are unfair. These are all very undesirable from a neuroscience perspective because people become less efficient, effective, and productive. Additionally, unhelpful memories and anchors can be set up, further reducing the impact an individual can have within an organization and the organization can have overall. I think Neil is incredibly perceptive, for many reasons including that what he believes is backed up by neuroscience.

NEIL MORRISON – HR DIRECTOR, RANDOM HOUSE GROUP

It is funny because the way we do HR and the way we manage in publishers is very different, and in some ways, if you went to some places they'd tell you it was old fashioned because it is all about individual touch, and it is all about connection and human-to-human relationships. I would actually argue that it is light years ahead. It is just taking time to look back and see what made people stay with organizations, what was really valuable to them, what have we lost through the homogenization of organizations and how do we get back to a place that feels better? A personal trophy moment of mind was after being here three or four years, I was at a Christmas dinner event and was sat next to someone I didn't know, and someone else introduced me, "this is Neil, he is the HR director" and this junior employee went, "I love getting emails from you because it is always something really exciting," and I thought how often do HR people get that versus "oh god, they're always telling us what we can't do." Our track record and our experience has always been that we communicate the negative messages to the individuals who need them. So if something goes wrong we don't send an email out to everyone saying, "It has come to our attention that this that and the other, grrrrr," and everyone goes, "ahh." You deal with the individual and where the problems are and focus on the positivity.

The culture is one of a very human passion. It is not very corporate and can seem a little chaotic. Beautifully organized in many ways but just doesn't look it to the naked eye. It is a culture of support and teamwork. People relate to each other not on hierarchy but on relationship so if you want to get things done you do so through relationships with others not because you are more senior. It can often seem like it is quite hard to get things done because you've got to talk to a gazillion people as opposed to talk to the boss who will tell everyone that they've got to do it.

It fosters a nice culture of people relating to each other that isn't just about work. So a lot of the conversations will be around family, holidays, food, or whatever it is, and people tend to know more about you as a person than any other organization I've ever worked with and actually be interested. So with my team, when they join and they have induction I tell them, "Don't tell them who you are and what you've done, just go and ask them questions about themselves. What are they publishing, how long have they been here, how did they get into it, where do they live, have they got kids." It's all those sorts of things that create that culture so in some ways it is more like a large slightly strange and dysfunctional family that is spread over many generations and many families but ultimately it makes a very positive culture. It isn't blame-y, it is very supportive, sometimes a little too supportive in some ways. So very human I'd say.

ANDREA CARTWRIGHT – GROUP HR DIRECTOR, SUPERGROUP

We're pretty good at parties actually, as you could imagine. Yeah, so we have a big Christmas do, the stores do it regularly. For the more privileged of us, every time we launch a new season, we have a catwalk show and there is a big party that sits around that. One of the things that I think we are less good at is celebrating the success in between. So, trying to get people to do what I call spontaneous recognition with Thank You, have the afternoon off, finish out earlier, we are less good at and it's almost as if we need to help people think about doing that kind of thing. Because actually the Thank You's are really powerful. I've been trying to get the executive team to think about it actually and I sent them all a little recognition thing that said, "Thank you very much for doing this." Actually a few of them received it and I did it just before a meeting where we were going to discuss this stuff and said, "How much did each of you like getting your card?" And they were like, "It's so nice..." and that is how we need to make our people feel. Often it's not big things. We did a very, very good summer and autumn season last year and we sent, completely by surprise, every single one of our employees £100 worth of gift vouchers about two weeks before Christmas, and I have to say that the response was phenomenal. People were on Twitter talking about it, "Oh my god, I didn't expect this," so you do set yourself up for future years but there is something[...]You have to remember that to a lot of our staff that's more than they earn in a week, because they only work a few days a week for us or a few evening shifts and we make the decision that everybody gets £100 pounds. I have thought that is really, really important.

What's the Bottom Line?

The opportunity is to help shape a culture that values the humanness of people rather than force them to be different people inside and outside of work.

What Can I Do Today?

TRUST someone.

What Can I Put in Place for the Long Term?

- Trainings on TRUST.
- TRUST ambassadors.
- Start the real discussions around what sort of organization you want to be and whether you are prepared to do what it takes.
- A new organizational structure (that one probably not in your lunch hour).

What Is the Overall Ideal Vision?

An organization whose culture supports the individuals to be at their best. It really is that simple.

part IV
How Do We Manage People?

We don't actually manage people. We manage environments, systems, and processes. Think about what you are really looking for when you are after well-managed individuals. You ultimately want results. We know that behaviors get you those results. Trying to manage people person-to-person can get messy, tricky, and create problems. Of course it can also be rewarding, uplifting, and enrich people's days. When asked about management, most people's first thoughts, often only thoughts, go to this person-to-person approach. At Synaptic Potential one of our focuses when we work with organizations is the effect that the environment and culture has on people's behavior because it is often very influential.

As Peter Drucker said, we lead people, we manage things!

LOUISA FRYER - L&D, CATH KIDSON

How do people get managed? Sometimes I think that people don't give enough feedback, and I think that is a problem. I think that they don't do it because of a fear of conflict and a lack of training. With the training, perhaps the balance isn't quite there yet, or maybe it is but it's not in a credible kind of way. I think there is a bit of a negative stroke that happens and that is a lot of what I'm addressing in my training. Feedback is quite powerful, quite simple if you get it and then it's about building esteem. It should always be about building esteem or keeping esteem intact. If you lose your esteem, that is it, you are out, and then it's really hard to put people back when they have gone. There are pockets of people getting it in a way that it builds and it helps, and people getting it delivered in way that it doesn't. I think that it just depends on your role in the business, but it's changing, it's getting better everywhere. With a lack of consistent leadership framework or consistent values going well it's very hard to have a consistency and hoping you'll get managed and dealt with.

Depending on the results you are looking for you may choose to prioritize certain things over others. Let's consider how the environment can shape some behaviors.

ANGELA O'CONNOR – HR LOUNGE

I've always struggled a bit with management because I think people come to work as adults, they have lives at home, in their communities, they manage families, they manage finances, they manage their politics and religion, and then they come in to a workplace and we attempt to manage them sometimes. And that allows people to revert back into a parent/child scenario. So I see things completely differently. My interest is always in the grace of individuals and also in them being responsible for their own growth. [...] In an organization, you have a lot of knowledge and resource available; you can do something. Sometimes it is just about tapping in to that and giving people explicit permission to work at their own issues, and sometimes it is charging them with accountability and genuinely trying to make decisions. I've always worked from that perspective; it's much more about the freedom of individuals rather than the management of individuals. But then, I've been doing this a long time, so I've worked through the insecurities of being a first-time line manager and feeling as if you need to know all the answers and that you should be able to solve every problem and be in control of everything; 30 years later you stop doing that.

9

Your Fundamental Checklist for Behavioral Success

Why people behave the way they do is a question with deep importance to organizations. There are many closely related influencers of our behavior. We can step back and become aware of three core things:

1. Is this a hot or cold network thing?
2. Is a threat or reward being registered?
3. What is grabbing their attention?

The answers to this fundamental checklist will give you a huge lead on how to go on to shape behaviors the way you want them. Let's have a look at each of these concepts before moving into some applications. Trying to change behaviors without really having an idea of what is causing them can be a tricky thing to do. We see many organizations wasting time, money, and energy changing things that don't address the core reasons why people are behaving the way they are. Consider behaviors that concern safety. It would seem natural to most people that individuals would want to remain safe while at work. However many organizations see challenges with adherence to safety policies. Changing this behavior is not normally as simple as sending out an email reminding people of the policy – if only!

Hot and Cold Network

The hot and cold network has also been described as System 1 and System 2, or the implicit system and the explicit system. Daniel Kahneman has raised the profile of this area of research wonderfully in recent years. In his book *Thinking, Fast and Slow*, he describes two systems. System 1 works automatically, quickly, with little or no effort and no sense of voluntary control. System 2 involves effortful mental activities and is associated with subjective experiences of concentration and choice.[1] Both systems are important and both have different capabilities. We think of System 2 as being in control. Many organizations are set up as if this is solely the case. We tend to believe that the conscious, rational, reasoning part of us is considering things, evaluating options, and making decisions. Sometimes this is the case. However System 1 is actually at work far more prevalently than we give it credit for. The automatic processing and generating of impressions and feelings is going on under our conscious radar. Most of the time, the two systems work together very well. The cooperation means that we can be highly efficient by minimizing effort.

From the neuroscientific literature we can see parallels with the hot and cool networks. The research comes from various different angles, so to get an overall appreciation we need to throw it all out there and then make sense of it. Emotional processing involves the amygdala, posteromedial orbital cortex, and ventral anterior cingulate cortex. Activity decreases in these areas during some attention-demanding cognitive tasks. Similarly during some emotional states, we see a decrease in areas such as the dorsal anterior cingulate and dorsolateral prefrontal cortex that are linked to cognitive function.[2] We see two separate systems at work in a variety of different experiments. The system that involves parts of the limbic system associated with the midbrain dopamine system, including the paralimbic cortex is preferentially activated by decisions that involve immediately available rewards.[3]

Interestingly we see interaction between emotional processing on reasoning. The right lateral prefrontal cortex (rlPFC) is activated when a person inhibits a prepotent response associated with belief-bias and correctly completes a logical task. This fits with the rlPFC's role in cognitive monitory. On the flip side, when belief-bias overcomes logic we see involvement of the ventral medial PFC (important in affective processing).[4]

Further evidence for these two networks comes from looking at cognitive interference by emotional distraction. Goal-oriented behavior can be disrupted by emotional distracters. When volunteers were working on a delayed-response working memory task, the areas of their brain that were active were observed. During the delay period the dorsolateral prefrontal cortex (dlPFC) and lateral parietal cortex (lPC) were active. When emotional distracters were presented, the emotional processing regions of the brain became active, the amygdala and ventrolateral prefrontal cortex. Simultaneously the dlPFC and lPC became deactivated and the working memory performance was impaired. This is another example of the cold executive system interacting with the hot ventral system involved in emotional processing.[5]

Imagine we want to get someone to do something within an organization. The most prevalent approach to achieving this outcome is to ask people to do the thing. If that doesn't work, an email reminder may be issued. Still no luck? Perhaps a change of policy is required. All of these approaches try to utilize System 2, our rational, logical system. The hope is that we receive the information, process it, and then act accordingly. People trying to tap into System 2 presume that because something "makes sense" that we will do it. We are far more complex than that and so relying on action based on what is perceived as making sense misses big chunks of what really motivates people.

Habits

A colleague of mine (a neuroscientist working in the behavioral change field) recently suggested that a goal for organizations might be to embed new behaviors as habits. To go from utilizing the cool network to the hot network to conserve energy and free up the cool network for other things. It would be sensible to utilize the hot networks to create these new neural pathways that could make the behavior more instinctual in the future. Being aware of the habits you are intentionally or unintentionally conditioning within people could be a valuable audit.

Attention

Your attention is one of your most valuable assets. Where people's attention is being paid forms a big part of shaping their brain, subsequently their behaviors, and then their results. We are often blissfully unaware of where our attention is, and subsequently what we are missing. The famous gorilla experiment, showing how we can be effectively "blind" to objects or details we don't expect to see, has been developed over the years. One of my favorite developments is the one that preyed on unsuspecting radiologists. As you are probably aware, radiologists spend *years* honing their ability to detect small abnormalities in specific types of images. Their brain is carefully wired to do this job after years of training. In one experiment, 24 radiologists performed a routine lung-nodule detection task where they looked for abnormalities. An image of a gorilla, 48 times the size of the average nodule, was added to a test case – 83 percent of the radiologists failed to spot the gorilla. Eye tracking showed that the majority of radiologists even looked directly at where the gorilla was "hiding." This showed that even experts are vulnerable to inattentional blindness.[6]

What do you want people to focus their attention on? Chances are, they too will suffer from inattentional blindness.

One group of researchers proposed that boredom is linked to attention. They say that the aversive state of boredom occurs when we:

a) Are not able to successfully engage attention with internal (thoughts or feelings) or external (environmental stimuli) information required for participating in satisfying activity.

b) Are focused on the above.

c) Attribute the cause of the boredom to the environment.

Boredom can be a big problem. Avoiding it is another reason to enhance our ability to engage minds at work.[7]

Behavioral Hacks

So what are some of the ways to work with the external environment to act on the hot network?

Nudging is one approach. "Nudges are ways of influencing choice without limiting the choice set or making alternatives appreciably more costly in terms of time, trouble, social sanctions, and so forth. They are called for because of flaws in individual decision-making, and they work by making use of those flaws."[8] We wouldn't frame what we're looking at here as *flaws in decision making*, rather that nudges can utilize *different* decision-making networks. The science behind nudging has been embraced in various ways by the British Cabinet Office, the government of New South Wales, and President Obama.

One of the challenges raised against the practice of nudging is that it isn't linked to long-term behavior changes. There is not the data available to make widespread conclusions on this front. However, our approach is to encourage and equip organizations to utilize all the great scientifically underpinned ways forward we have. A nudge may work wonderfully alongside an education piece or strategies to embed new behaviors neurally.

Classic examples of nudges include the urinals in Amsterdam's airport. The challenge was that poor aim was making the restrooms undesirable to use. While many things could have been done, for example putting a sign up asking men to be more careful, employing more cleaners to clear up, or charging sloppy men, instead a nudge was employed. This was very cheap, very easy, and very successful in reducing spillage by

80 percent. What did they do? Simply placed the image of a black fly just to the left of the drain within the urinal. As it happens, if you give men a target, they aim at it.[9]

Influences on Behavior

There is not space to go through in detail all the many ways our judgment and behavior is influenced, however it is important to cover some contributors here. It is here we dance into the world of behavioral sciences to draw some valuable insights.[10]

The aim is to consider the LANDSCAPE FOR creating behaviors. Here are some to be aware of.

Loss

Anchoring

Norms

Default

Salience

Commitments

Ambassador

Priming

Emotion

Feedback

Optimism

Reward

Let's have a slightly deeper look at what each of these influencers are and some of the effects they typically have. We are still just scratching the surface and undergoing one of our workshops to really grasp these concepts and understand how to flexibly apply them to your organization is the best next step if you are keen to create sustainable behavior change.

Loss

"Losses loom larger than gains," it has been said.[11] Might this have something to do with a dopamine dip when something we expect is taken away? Maybe. Certainly it can be useful to be aware of concepts such as the endowment effect, where on average people need to be paid twice as much to give up something than they would be willing to pay to get it initially. We want to be aware of people's emotional attachment to things. This is useful to be aware of as a shaper of behavior. At times it may be useful to make people aware of the potential impact it could be having on behavior.

Examples

The effect of not providing an annual expected bonus may hit people hard. Consider what or where people are coming from when they are joining a new organization. What are they giving up? When roles change, if there is a perceived loss it can impact behavior beyond what may be considered rational.

Anchoring

What are people anchored to? What has the person been exposed to that could influence their decision making now? Anchoring bias is a process whereby people are influenced by specific information given before a judgment. There is robust evidence that this is powerful.[12] When anchors have a numerical value they may be completely unrelated to a following question, and yet still exert an irrational influence. A landmark study rigged a roulette wheel. It was programmed to land on either 65 (high) or 10 (low). The participants were then asked if that was more or less than the proportion of African member states in the UN. They finally were asked to guess the exact proportion. It was found that those given the higher anchor (the "random" 65) made higher estimates subsequently. The median was 45 percent for those anchored to 65, and only 25 percent for those anchored to 10.

In another experiment, this time with CEOs, similar findings were reported. After being primed with an anchor (either high or low) they were then asked to estimate the price of a bottle of whiskey. Their guesses varied by around £13 (170 Kroner).[13]

Examples

Costs of things are an obvious example. How long things may take to do is another. Consider the implications for an organization in negotiations. If a high anchor point is set, through whatever means, it makes it more likely a final figure will be agreed that is higher than if a low anchor point had been set.

Norms

Other people's behavior can have a big impact on what we do. The culture can obviously be hugely important in an organization. Investing time in changing what the majority of people do can sometimes create enough momentum to make a big impact. In an effort by the UK nudge-unit to minimize the no shows for doctor's appointments they utilized norms. Initially they asked patients to commit to attending. This resulted in an 18 percent reduction in no shows. When they showed a descriptive norm, *X out of Y show up for their appointment*, this decreased the no shows to 33 percent.

In another experiment, households were to be nudged into reducing their energy expenditure. One group received their normal energy statement. The second group received in addition information about the average consumption of their neighbors. The third group received the same as the second group and in addition information demonstrating how to change their usage. The third group achieved twice the reduction of the second – a total of 9 percent. This behavior change lasted longer too.[14]

A note here – stick to the truth.

Examples

Consider the norms in your organization. Do most people normally take a lunch break? Do most people get to work in a healthy or environmentally friendly way? Do people choose to initiate mentoring relationships with juniors? Do people share their learning experiences with colleagues after training? If you're looking to change the behavior of the minority then sharing what the majority do could be a good way forward.

to change the behavior of the minority then sharing what the majority do could be a good way

Default

We naturally tend to go with the pre-set option.[15, 16] We are predictably lazy most of the time. Compare the percentages of adults registered as organ donors in countries such as France, Portugal, and Poland – all over 90 percent, with countries such as Denmark, the UK, and Germany – all under 20 percent. What's the difference? An opt-out system versus an opt-in system.

Examples

What are your defaults? For example, what is your pensions default? Are your email system defaults such that emails go through to people 24/7? What are the defaults in your induction processes for new hires? Do you have defaults for your clients? Anywhere there is a pre-set option, or there could be, there is an opportunity to be considered.

Salience

Our attention is drawn by novelty and relevance. The litter bins that glow in the dark attract our attention and reduce litter on the streets. The chocolate bars at the counter where we are paying are relevant (if we like chocolate). The alert that pops up when we have a new email definitely is salient.

Examples

What is salient in the environment in which people work? If people knew how to adapt their environment so they were more in control of what they wanted to have grab their attention that could be helpful. The scope here is incredibly wide.

Commitments

We try to do what we publicly say we will. Often we struggle to do things we know are good for us or that we even say we want to do, for example, taking exercise. If a goal is publicly stated, then the potential reputational damage of not doing it often shapes behavior. The involvement of money in a commitment has also been shown to make people more likely to do something.[17]

Examples

People often pledge a fundraising goal, perhaps to run a 10k race and raise money. It is more likely they will achieve this goal if they have publicly declared their intention. Inviting people to write down and publicly share their commitments, for example how they will behave at work, what their goals are, learning intentions, people they will connect with, and so on, could also be powerful.

Ambassador

Who is positioning and sharing any message? What is their position within the message receivers' minds? How are they related to the people receiving the message? Who are all the different options to deliver a message?

Examples

If a new initiative is being rolled out, is it best that the CEO is involved in supporting it, or not? If a message is going out to clients, is it best to come from a leader within the organization, or another high-profile client?

Priming

Subconscious cues can have powerful effects on our behavior. Words, sights, and smells have all been shown to influence behavior. The next time you are in a canteen, have a sniff – if there is the scent of an all-purpose cleaning product then you are more likely to keep your table clean![18] The classic priming experiments that use words linked to the elderly then show people walk more slowly between rooms are fascinating.[19] Equally, priming people with words linked to fitness made people more likely to use the stairs in place of the lifts.[20] If I show you a smiley face you may drink more than if I show you a frowning face.[21]

Examples

Think about the words and images that people are surrounded by. What is on the walls, can you change it regularly? Do you have different spaces priming for different states or behaviors? Consider where you meet clients. What effect could the environment be having on them?

Emotion

Our emotional response to ideas or situations can affect our behavior. We often find ourselves doing things without having consciously decided to do so. It makes sense that different cocktails of chemicals soaring around our brain and body affect our behavior. This is one of the reasons we want people to feel excited on Mondays and fulfilled on Fridays. How we feel about and at work has an effect on how we work.

Examples

Utilize the element of surprise in making people feel a certain way. Consider how the environment may influence how people feel and how they behave as a result.

Feedback

Feedback can affect behavior. If we can see how many steps we have taken during a day we may be motivated to do more (to achieve a goal) or discouraged if we're miles off the goal. Our brain gives us feedback in terms of whether or not something is matching with our expectations and whether the reward networks are activated or not.

Examples

If people are starting to change behaviors feeding back the positive steps and results, especially in terms of what it means to them, may serve as a motivator to continue that behavior. Feedback may be publicly given or privately given by an individual. Feedback may be a self-reflection-based process.

Optimism

The optimism bias is subtly at work affecting our behaviors. In our personal lives it may make us less likely to get a health check-up (thinking a serious illness won't happen to us). However, being optimistic can help lower stress and improve physical health.[22] Looking at people's brains showed that the more optimistic a person is the higher the activity in the amygdala and rostral anterior cingulated cortex when imagining positive future events, relative to negative ones. Also there was stronger connectivity between the two brain structures. Depressed people show abnormal activity in these two regions. Healthy people tend to think things are better than they are, mildly depressed people tend to get it about right, and severely depressed people expect things to be worse than reality.[23]

Examples

At work how optimistic we are may affect whether we go for a promotion. It may affect how much effort we put into proposals or networking or working with colleagues. Perhaps the added effort optimistic people put in may end up changing the results for the better. If your team is primed with positivity and optimism then their performance is likely to be better.

Reward

How does this behavior reward the individual? This is an area that normally requires digging. When we work with managing directors this is often a very valuable breakthrough when they realize the benefits that people have been getting from doing the undesirable behavior and that it is that which will need to change. When we think of rewards from a neuroscience perspective we are considering the activation of the reward networks within the brain. This may or may not be something people are consciously aware of.

Examples

In one organization we worked with, the simple challenge of people wearing headphones in an area where clients would see them, and the managing director felt, giving the wrong impression, was better understood when he considered the reward wearing headphones gave them. They were better able to concentrate with the headphones on. They were less likely to be interrupted. They were subsequently better able to do their job. Hearing this, the managing director changed his approach. Rather than going to them and again telling them off, and emailing them to ask them to stop doing it, he reconsidered. He realized the unconscious pull of getting good work done was more rewarding to them than adhering to a new rule. In this instance, a change in the environment to facilitate uninterrupted work was the better long-term approach and more likely to lead to the overall desired result.

the unconscious pull of getting good work done was more rewarding to them than adhering to a new rule

A dirty kitchen could be a result of people wanting to be quick and get back to work. They leave their unwashed cup telling themselves that they need to push on. Perhaps not being seen washing up boosts their ego by thinking they are too important to wash up.

Combinations

As you'll have seen through some of the examples, the potential when you combine behavioral influences can dramatically improve the overall result. Of course we are still learning how different things work. Both surprising and predictable behavioral changes occur when we tweak environments. Think about what your workplace smells like…could it be having a behavioral affect?[16] It may also be useful to consider the frame that is shared in moving towards a goal. Studies have shown that individuals are more motivated if their attention is direction to whichever is smaller in size, the accumulated or remaining progress.[24]

What's the Bottom Line?

You can powerfully influence behavior in ways other than the carrot-and-stick approach.

What Can I Do Today?

Check out your LANDSCAPE FOR creating a behavior you want to shape.

What Can I Put in Place for the Long Term?

Systems to explore the LANDSCAPE FOR creating desirable behaviors.

What Is the Overall Ideal Vision?

Organizations who consider the unconscious influences on people's behavior and utilize more sophisticated ways to support people to do the jobs they want to do.

chapter 10

Managing for...

In this chapter we look at the alternative approach to management. While we're not pushing you as far out of your comfort zone as to suggest that you have to get rid of any hierarchy, that there should be no bosses (although that certainly is an option), we *are* suggesting a different mindset and approach. Instead of managers being trained to manage people, we suggest that they are trained to shape the environment and the systems and to be aware of what people can do personally. These are the headings we explore under each concept.

Manage for Happiness

Why Bother?

It may surprise you to hear that something as familiar to most of us as happiness is in its infant stage of research from a neuroscience perspective.[1] However, psychology and other disciplines have gathered a lot of data that suggests we need to pay attention to people's happiness. It is widely accepted that happy people:

- Work better with others
- Have more energy

• Are more creative, optimistic, motivated, and healthy
• Worry less about making mistakes
• Learn quicker
• Make better decisions

Ultimately, with lower absenteeism, lower staff turnover, and increased productivity organizations with happier people are more profitable.[2]

Measuring stuff

Lots of organizations are trying to measure various different things. It always tickles me to see how much weight is placed on what comes out of the research. The answers we give to survey-type questions are extremely easy to influence. For example, the order of the questions that you ask can influence the response someone gives. Place a question about someone's political views before asking about life satisfaction and you get an effect almost as big as becoming unemployed.[3] Outside of work, if you are asked about your marital satisfaction and then your life satisfaction it influences your answer. Statistically we see higher correlations between marital and life satisfactions if the questions follow in that order than if the life satisfaction question comes first.[4]

What Is Happiness?

We can think of happiness as having three components: pleasure, meaning, and engagement, related to feelings of commitment and participation in life.[5] Scientists believe that our affective reactions such as pleasure have objective features. This means that affective neuroscience can identify objective aspects of pleasure reactions and better understand the underpinning brain substrates.[6] Affect is more than the way we feel, more than the subjective experience of emotion. It is also the objective aspects of behavioral, physiological, and neural reactions.[7]

There are many aspects to happiness. One neuropsychological theory proposes that many of the positive influences positive affect has on cognitive tasks are associated with increased dopamine. Improvements seen in the consolidation of long-term memories, working memory, and creative problem solving could all be linked to dopamine. When more dopamine is released, our cognitive flexibility increases which can lead to better creative problem solving.[8]

Environment

Every workplace is different and needs to fulfill certain practical requirements. Can someone be happy in a factory environment? Yes. Can someone be happy in an office? Yes. Can someone be happy working in a field? Yes. So this section is simply to stimulate thought, a tailored approach is vital.

Attention

We have a natural negative bias meaning that we will focus on negative things and ruminate around them instead of the positives. The power of this is great so it takes an individual strength and rewiring to make it easier to move on from negative thoughts. Organizations can make the environment as happiness inducing as possible, to help people guide their own attention back to things that put them in a more positive state. One large bakery we worked with had pictures of happy team members at work all around the building. Context is important.

Music

Music is powerful.[9] It can affect our autonomic nervous system and our subjective feelings.[10] It is a little out there, however an organization with a space for music making (the next stage on from music listening) could have very positive effects on individuals and teams. Capital One, a UK-based credit card company won "Best Workplace" in 2013. It has a fully equipped music room. In some countries and workplaces, it is normal to sing together during the workday. In schools it is normal. Recent competitions in the UK have encouraged groups to form groups from within the organization and practice together in the hope of being named "the best workplace choir." This is great – the next step could be to have a space with instruments that people could pick up and play together. Music can bring people together, elevate mood, encourage creativity, and a state of flow.

Music can bring people together

Exercise

Michael Otto, psychology professor, says, "The link between exercise and mood is pretty strong. Usually within five minutes after moderate exercise you get a mood-enhancement effect."[11] You can't make people exercise, but you can make it easier for them if they choose to. Consider:

- Having showers at work and a place to change
- Having a bicycle storage area
- Running an exercise class in-house at lunchtime
- Running an after work yoga class

James Blumenthal, a clinical psychologist, says, "There's good epidemiological data to suggest that active people are less depressed than inactive people." In one of his studies with people with major depressive disorder, exercise was of comparable help to people as antidepressants.[11] Depressed and anxious people tend to be less happy, so with exercise delivering real benefits in these areas, too, it makes even more sense to facilitate exercise where possible.

Systems

Happy culture

Of course people are not going to be happy all the time. That would be false and is not desirable. However, creating a culture where people really hear the good things and internalize them into good experiences and allow that to shape their brains – that is desirable. Something as simple as complimenting or thanking someone for a piece of work they did can be harnessed. Rather than letting a person brush it off (as sometimes happens) encourage people to own the good things they do and feel good about it. When a team does well then anchoring that practically and neurologically is important. Have a 15-minute party with hats and cake and then put one of the hats on a shelf to remember the experience by. Alternatively write down something you are grateful to a team member for during the project and put them all in a box to be delivered to the individuals later that day.

Exercise

Even if the environment isn't well set up for exercise there are still things that can be done to encourage it. Creating a board with the days of the week running along the top and spaces for people to write their names down the side can help to nudge. Different stickers could be placed on the chart to indicate exercise sessions people have completed. Perhaps even a column where they could draw how they felt after the session would be useful.

A "core club" that meets for just 20 minutes twice a week doesn't need much space, a change of clothes, or a shower afterwards. The group can just gather and work on core strength together. A "running club" could meet after work and people could go home afterwards to shower.

Personal

How happy are your friends?

Over time the happiness of those around us can affect us. How are the people in close physical proximity to you feeling? Three degrees of separation can have an effect (similarly to depression, anxiety, loneliness, drinking, eating exercise, and so on). Examining the state of people you spend most time with may be useful.[12]

Manage for Quality Thinking

What Is Quality Thinking?

Quality thinking is a core skill. Almost all jobs could benefit from quality thinking, even the highly repetitive ones. Organizations that value quality thinking and have systems in place to listen to the thoughts employees have are further along than those who believe people are just there to do a job (not to think). Quality thinking has typically been thought of as requiring the prefrontal cortex to be active. This type of analytical, logical, rational thinking is still very important. Our executive functions and ability to process lots of information consciously is prevalent in the workplace and justly valued. On the flip side of the coin, we have the type of processing that has not got the widespread recognition it deserves. This is the method that utilizes the implicit system. You'll remember that the implicit system involves the basal ganglia and in the state of flow requires the lowering of activity within the prefrontal cortex. Dopamine is important for all quality thinking. It helps us to focus and to want to do more of this.

Environment

Whether you are aiming for the prefrontal cortex to be in full swing or the hypofrontality needed for the flow state, you don't want any distractions around for quality thinking. People will be cultivating intensely focused attention, trying to get into the zone. Each time they are distracted, be that by a deliberate interruption from a colleague, by someone else's phone ringing, or by something salient coming into their awareness (like a passerby with a big cake) it takes time and effort to return to that focused state. An environment that facilitates long periods of uninterrupted concentration is hugely valuable.

Systems

Working with open plan

For some organizations we've worked with the news that an open plan office design isn't as desirable as they'd been led to believe is a bit of a blow. If that is all you have and you still want people to be able to try to get into a state of flow or into some deep executive faculty style thinking then you can utilize systems to help. One organization allowed people to wear noise-blocking headphones so they could block out auditory interruptions. Another had little signs that people could put on their desks or on their cubicles that said "Brain at Work" along with a time they were taking a break. It almost goes without saying that turning off email alerts and phones is key. It may even be worth experimenting with protecting a couple of hours within an organization where everyone knows it is "Brain Power Hours" when everyone puts their heads down on concentrated work. Afterwards the normal scurrying around asking questions and collaborating resumes.

Growth mindset

The mindset you have is important to your ability to think and process information. It is also important to your ability to get into flow. If "you believe that you can develop yourself, then you're open to accurate information about your current abilities, even if it's unflattering," shares Carol Dweck.[13] In order to learn effectively you need to be okay with the reality of the situation. Many people are not strong enough to hear the truth, from themselves or anyone else. Feedback has to be given dressed up so much we don't actually understand what it means. An ideal situation is one where people can acknowledge where they are at, and realize that can change.

The flow of flow

Internal systems need to support the flow of flow. Consider four stages proposed by Benson:[14]

1. Struggle
2. Release
3. Flow
4. Recovery

While the stage's names may be a little interesting, the process will resonate with many people. The first stage is a loading phase where you gather information, analyze problems, or study. During this phase cortisol, adrenaline, and norepinephrine may be released. It can feel tough during this stage (certainly not like you're in flow). This process involves us assimilating information consciously in order to turn it into chunks we can store to recall unconsciously later. Perseverance and an understanding of what is occurring here is important.

The second stage is one commonly skipped or unintentionally discouraged in organizations. Where time is precious and people are rewarded based on results this stage feels counterintuitive (because most people haven't mentally uploaded the chunks that would make it a really logical next step). The essence of this stage is to relax. To take a break. The idea is that nitric oxide increases, causing the stress hormones to decrease and subsequently dopamine and endorphins to increase.

The third stage is flow – which feels like flow. The fourth stage is recovery. It makes sense to capitalize on the experience that has just occurred. Lock in the memories and lessons. Having a little headspace time after a time of flow is useful to regenerate ready for the next intensive period.

a little headspace time after a time of flow is useful

Blended learning

There has been a lot of interest around blended learning, 70:20:10, and so on, recently. The reality is that we have always been learning outside a training room. We are social beings. We can learn a lot from one another. Strategically creating times where people can come together and work through ideas, sharing experiences and knowledge they've gained elsewhere has lots of benefits. It helps the individuals sharing to process and cement what it is they are sharing. It widens the listeners' experience and gives them more patterns to draw upon in the future. You could hold a book club, a snack-and-share session, a cross departmental picnic, or something more imaginative! Anything that brings people together to learn from each other can lead to a higher quality of thinking afterwards.

Personal

We each have to assume responsibility for minimizing distractions. Turning off email alerts, any mobiles, putting signs up indicating we're in "quality thinking" mode are all strategies down to us. Remember from Chapter 5 (The Jarring Awakening) some of the keys to getting into a state of flow:

We each have to assume responsibility for minimizing distractions

1. Clear goals
2. Immediate feedback
3. Challenge/skills ratio

These keys help release dopamine, which helps you focus and so can improve your quality thinking.

Manage for Great Decisions

Great decisions come in many shapes and sizes. Again, looking for a one strategy fits all is unlikely to suffice. However there are some strong indicators that point us in the direction of solid considerations to make. We know that great decisions can be the result of information from the implicit or the explicit system.

What Are Intuitions?

Intuitions can be described as "affectively-charged judgements that arise rapidly, involuntarily and non-consciously on the basis of holistic associations."[15]

- Affective – there is a component that can be characterized by that "gut feeling," this can be interpreted by the intensity and feeling to be more "approach" or "avoid" in nature.
- Uninvited – intuition doesn't need an invitation, it crops up unexpectedly and instantaneously.
- Parallel-process driven – information is drawn from multiple streams, processed without our conscious awareness, and delivers big picture insights.

Environment

As we saw in the previous chapter, nudges can influence the decisions we make – as can biases. In practice, this means that we may want to try to raise our awareness of any nudges and biases that could be influencing our decision-making process. The next section is a practical way to help do this.

Mindful decisions

People who utilize mindfulness techniques can make great decisions.[16] The internal environment (the brain) is functionally connected in a way that supports the individual. Mindfully considering which decisions actually need to be made, assessing the information that needs to be acquired and processed, learning from feedback, and coping with any result are all potentially strengthened in a mindful person. The process tends to be slower, but the implementation faster. If you want more mindful individuals then creating a space at work where people are reminded to invest five minutes in a meditation could help create more mindful brains and more mindful approaches even when not in that environment. A classic example is to have chairs in a quiet area with headphones linked to iPods with a selection of meditations. A cheaper alternative is a beanbag!

Emotion contagion

It may be worthwhile being aware of who else is around when a decision is being made. It has been shown that it is easy to be affected by another person's emotional state.[17] Since we also know that emotional states can influence decision making this is pertinent. If time is not a pressure then potentially "sitting with" a decision for a period before enacting it may enable you to see how you feel about it once the influence has disappeared. However, in meetings when this isn't the norm another strategy may be required.

Implicit decisions – solo

If a decision may be made best by the implicit system then it is useful to have:

- Clear goals
- Immediate feedback
- Appropriate challenge/skill ratio

So checking in that the environment is supporting these will help a person get into flow and focus their attention. The goals need to be super clear. They need to be bite-size chunks. The big picture goal is unhelpful because at this point because it draws the person out of the now. The same applies to the feedback. Immediate means not waiting for a manager to do it. It can't even wait for sales figures or trial results. The goal needs to be formed in a way that immediate feedback is possible. We need the explicit system to be able to go offline, so to speak, to allow the decisions to be made elsewhere.

Systems

Collective decision making – group flow

Often decisions are not made alone. From a neuroscience perspective things get much more complex when we consider several brains all working on something together. The potential is also very exciting though because rather than just one individual's pattern recognition at work you have that multiplied. Also you add in some novelty from other's experience and this can help stimulate further. The underpinning considerations are the same as trying to create individual flow with just a couple of extras, this is basic stuff but many organizations do not prioritize things being this way:

- *Shared clear goals* – As always you need clarity so you know when you've arrived, while also having enough scope to be creative on how you get there.
- *Good communication* – Flow can be easily blocked by poor communication. A good way to remember the helpful approach is to (1) listen, (2) accept, (3) add. Avoid blocking people or negating what people say. Accept it and add to it. The principles of Improvisation can be useful; work from what the last person left you with. By listening closely to what was said you'll help yourself stay focused and present.
- *Familiarity* – A common language and shared knowledge base speeds things up.
- *Equal participation and skill level* – Equal roles and similar skill levels are useful to reduce any threat response. That isn't to say everyone has

to have the same role within the organization, instead an equal role within the group that is getting into flow.

- *Risk* – This is easy to misinterpret. Flow researchers suggest that an element of risk can help people get into the state, too much, however, and it can paralyze groups. You don't want fear to overwhelm people, but risk that people can cope with can help focus attention.
- *Sense of control* – Autonomy and sense of competence over the task helps create flow.

Personal

Managing perceived risk

You know yourself best. You can get to know yourself better. To make great decisions you want to be able to pay attention to inputs but not get overwhelmed. You want to keep focused and part of that involves managing your brain. Practicing in and out of your place of work is ideal. Any opportunity can be a playground to strengthen the neural networks that will make you better at this. Next time there is a child's birthday party coming up – offer to help!

Managers and colleagues can support each other to grow in this way by having it on their radar. Checking in with people formally or informally to see what element of decision making they are working on can motivate people to try new things.

Lucy was asked what she thought HR was.

LUCY SENTENCE – HR BUSINESS PARTNER, MATHWORKS

That is really a good question and one that I've been actually wrestling with myself a little bit, over the last couple of months. [...] They hadn't had anybody here working at the UK business partner for a period of 18 months ... and there were some issues, in terms of the relationships and the level of trust between the managers and HR. So I've inherited a bit of baggage. I've had a lot of people saying, What are you here for? What is HR? What is an HR business partner? My answer is been, "It depends."

It depends very much on the context and the situation. HR is very broad in scope in many ways but I guess its main function is to help the talent and the input of its employees. It's a device to help manage the softer side of things that can't be dealt with by the process and the other elements of the working environment. It is really there to help leverage the people and help them maximize their performance and be prepared to meet the organization's changing needs.

Manage for Creative Output

What Is Creativity?

Gone are the days (aren't they?) where people said that the right brain was the creative brain, and the left-brain was all about logic. We have known for a long time that creativity is more complex than just involving one hemisphere of the brain. Let's consider the three main networks involved in creativity. The executive attention network is recruited when we need laser-like focus. It would be active when following a complex report, doing challenging problem solving or processing a presentation in a second language. It involves the lateral prefrontal cortex and posterior parietal lobe. The default mode network is important for constructing dynamic mental simulations: drawing on past experiences to imagine alternatives. It involves the medial prefrontal cortex and temporal lobe and communicates with areas of the parietal cortex. Finally the salience network monitors the external environment and the internal consciousness and flexibly passes our attention to whatever is most salient. It involves the dorsal anterior cingulate cortex and anterior insular.[18]

With creativity, different stages call for different networks and subsequently different management approaches. For example, initially you may want to imagine new possibilities – blue sky thinking as it were. During this time you want to reduce the executive attention network and increase default and salience network activation. When you want to then critique or implement ideas you'll need to up the involvement of the executive attention network.

Environment

Open plan office layout

Bearing in mind that there is never a one-size-fits-all approach that will always deliver, for creativity, your best bet is to at least have available an open space. This is an area where people can gather and sit together or move around together. The zone can invite people to move by having drink-making facilities, a water cooler, plants that may need attending to, even different types of seat to experiment with.

Rich, stimulating, flexible, tailored environment

This next suggestion is really an extension of the previous, an ideal. For most organizations it would need to be a space that was shared, although there are adaptations that can be made to incorporate some of the components even in a normal meeting room. This special space would have a range of stimulating prompts: sensory-rich activities, for example sand, playdough, music, white boards and different lighting options. Perhaps sharing different food together and catching up would be beneficial.

The space could be tailored to prime people by being able to put up particular images, words, or props. Consideration should be given to whether people need help focusing or help thinking laterally.

Mind wandering zone

Recent research has added weight to the experiential insight into how doing undemanding tasks can aid creativity. When compared with engaging in a demanding task, rest, or no break, we see that engaging in an undemanding task during an incubation period led to substantial improvements in performance.[19] Facilitating mind wandering can help facilitate creative problem solving. If the environment you're in doesn't have any undemanding tasks to hand, consider taking a break and going to the kitchen to do some washing up, watering the plants, or shredding some paper.

Facilitating mind wandering can help facilitate creative problem solving

Novelty, unpredictability and complexity

Of course the world outside of the office has a mass of environments that can stimulate creativity. A "rich environment" is made up of the components of novelty, unpredictability, and complexity. Novelty triggers dopamine and can mean danger or opportunity – both of which mean we want to pay attention. Unpredictability also means we want to pay attention, as does complexity. Where could you hold your next meeting?

JANE OLDS – HEAD OF HR, WEATHERBYS

How do I manage people for creative input or output? I think just through lots of encouragement. So through the review process we are trying to get people to feel more comfortable and more confident to give us their ideas and thoughts about how to make things better, how we can diversify our business. [...] One of the things that we have is what we call our High Achievers Club. Anybody that receives an "exceeded" review result goes in to this group of people that have a regular meeting on projects to work on, wide projects that involve the whole business. We find that by doing this it kind of lights up the creativity in these people and because they're often those that are ambitious and want to get on, it really gets them thinking and we get more out of them. We found through this initiative that we do get more ideas, from this group of people but not just from them; one-to-ones are conducted where managers are encouraging their staff to give ideas if they've got any, then people do come forward.

Systems

Neuropsychologist Barbara Sahakian says, "To really achieve anything, you have to be able to tolerate and enjoy risk. It has to become a challenge to look forward to. In all fields, to make exceptional discoveries you need risk – you're just never going to have a breakthrough without it." Being able to tolerate risk and the next stage of it actually being intrinsically rewarding is a central theme to creativity. This means that organizations that want more creativity need systems that don't penalize against risk taking. The nature of a risk is that there will be times where the result is great and times where it won't be. If your reward and recognition structure too harshly looks down upon loss of resources or loss of time then you may discourage creativity. Of course, the goal is normally a success; the challenge is just to manage the process (the systems) to get the balance of encouraging risk. Dopamine is released when people take risks. This enhances performance and increases pattern recognition.

Another big part of what is happening when we are creative is that pattern recognition. Being able to see patterns and then go lateral and pull in obscure thoughts, previous experiences, and memories is valuable. More dopamine is released during this time. In order to have a solid bank of patterns to then recognize it is important to strategically be uploading them into ourselves. Organizations can have many opportunities in place to aid this, for example:

1. Mentoring
2. Shadowing
3. Department swaps
4. Day with clients
5. Time with competitors

Personal

The state of flow is such an enjoyable one to be in we can seek it out for both personal and professional reasons. Ultimately, doing more of what we love means we are less likely to have regrets later in life. Choosing to spend time doing things out of work that offer novelty, unpredictability, or complexity can make it easier to get into the state of flow anytime (home or work). Going somewhere that triggers the state of awe is at the front end of flow. Consider a little stargazing or perhaps walk up a mountain to see the vastness below. In that moment most people take a deep breath, lose some self-consciousness, time is distorted and perhaps even experience a feeling that something bigger than oneself is present. Alternatively do something more active within nature. Work alongside the unpredictability of nature by kayaking or learning to surf. Even doing something as simple as changing your routines can trigger the release of dopamine and norepinephrine. Brush your teeth with the other hand. Cook something different for dinner (work your way around the world experimenting with different flavors!).

something as simple as changing your routines can trigger the release of dopamine

Deep embodiment

Getting into a state of deep embodiment is a skill that becomes easier with practice. It is about becoming fully aware of your body. You are aiming to tune into, turn up if you like, all the sensory input that is coming into your awareness. This is a process that is done best by the implicit system. When the explicit system gets involved the effectiveness decreases. When the reticular-activating system is engaged, implicit information processing is facilitated. Next the prefrontal cortex's higher order functions are disengaged. This is partly due to resource limitation. The benefit of the explicit system and emotional processes being quietened is that the implicit system can function optimally.[20] Exercise and sports are great ways to trigger deep embodiment, but so too are meditation practices. Or for the kid in you hopscotch or ladder drills can help improve proprioception and vestibular awareness. As do martial arts, tai chi, and yoga – so your choices are wide.

Personal flow hacks

• *Examine what you know.* Your knowledge is influencing how you think and what you come up with.

- *Get into a good state.* Support your divergent and spontaneous thinking, avoid those negative states.
- *Dedicate time to improving.*

Some organizations are enjoying fantastic creative output from their teams. Others are frequently left complaining that things are substandard.

I think it comes down to trust and credibility and the managers recognizing that they cannot have a one-sided approach. They need to understand the individual members on their team and how to get the best out of them, and how to also modify their style not just depending on the person but also depending on what's going on with that person. It's a performance management culture here and managers are really encouraged and helped to develop and give them the tools to be able to provide direction where it is needed and then shift for people [to be] fairly autonomous in their role. Being able to respond and just have that level of flexibility rather than kind of rigid "this is my style and this is what you'll get" [management approach].

Manage for Insights

What Are Insights?

Insights are those solutions that present themselves quickly and without warning.[21] There is normally a burst of gamma wave activity just before that "aha!" moment, and more activity in the temporal lobes and medial frontal cortex.[22] Insights don't necessarily need to happen every day. The process of making connections between things that previously eluded us makes us feel a sense of achievement.[23] When we think about insights, we want to consider:

- Stepping away from any problem or decision
- Getting into a good state

- Valuing time spent not thinking
- Investing in your brain uploads – ahead of needing your brain to link things up and make sense of things and produce an "aha!" moment.

Environment

One of the biggest pieces of advice to create insights would be to consider leaving the normal environment. You can go out of the office and go anywhere.

Helper's high

A great way to get out of your normal environment is to go and do something good for someone else. As discussed in Chapter 4 contributing has a range of benefits for you as well as those you help. The "helper's high" has also been linked to the state of flow.

Systems and Personal

Here are some general suggestions and information on which to base any systems or personal approaches

- Redirect your attention away from a problem. Allow your unconscious mind to wander, meander, search, and bring you back the answer you could have spent long hard hours thinking about and still not found.
- Value time spent not thinking. This could be the very time you are processing information and coming up with genius insights.
- Invest in your brain uploads. What you have put into your brain up to this point is what you then have access to process and join the dots between to come up with insights.
- Brainstorming has not been shown to be a good way to generate insights.
- Talk to some people with more experience and knowledge than you.
- There doesn't have to be an impasse before an insight, so don't get hung up on trying to create one!

What's the Bottom Line?

Using the environment, systems, and personal approaches can be effective enabling people to manage themselves.

What Can I Do Today?

Choose a behavior you want to change. Consider how you could adapt your environment, any systems, and your personal approach to increase the chances of you doing the new behavior. Remember to consider the implicit system's influence on you.

What Can I Put in Place for the Long Term?

Futuristic management ambassadors – individuals who have a responsibility to educate their peers about the different ways behaviors can be managed and encourage people to pioneer some of these new approaches.

What Is the Overall Ideal Vision?

The overall vision is to have organizations as equipped as possible to empower individuals to manage themselves. Enabling them to enjoy their work, contribute fully to the organization and for that to be reflected in the achievements of the company generally.

References

/ Introduction

1. Lawler III. E. E., Boudreau. J. W. (2012) *Effective Human Resource Management: A Global Analysis.* Stanford: Stanford University Press
2. Ulrich, D. and Brockbank, W. (2008) The business partner model: 10 years on: Lessons learned. *Human Resources Magazine.*
3. Laloux. F. (2014) *Reinventing Organizations: A Guide to Creating Organizations Inspired by the Next Stage of Human Consciousness.* Brussels: Nelson Parker

/ 1   The Beautifully Simple Model that Gets RESULTS

1. Klein, T. A., Ullsperger, M., Danielmeier, C. (2013). Error awareness and the insula: links to neurological and psychiatric diseases. *Frontiers in Human Neuroscience, 7,* 14. 10.3389/fnhum.2013.00014
2. Danielmeier C., Ullsperger M. (2011). Post-error adjustments. *Front. Psychol.* 2, 233. 10.3389/fpsyg.2011.00233
3. Craig A. D. (2011). Significance of the insula for the evolution of human awareness of feelings from the body. *Ann. N.Y. Acad. Sci.* 1225, 72–82. 10.1111/j.1749-6632.2011.05990.x
4. Craig A. D. (2009). How do you feel–now? The anterior insula and human awareness. *Nat. Rev. Neurosci.* 10, 59–70 10.1038/nrn2555
5. Menon V., Uddin L. Q. (2010). Saliency, switching, attention and control: A network model of insula function. *Brain Struct. Funct.* 214, 655–667. 10.1007/s00429-010-0262-0
6. Wessel J. R., Danielmeier C., Morton J. B., Ullsperger M. (2012). Surprise and error: Common neuronal architecture for the processing of errors and novelty. *J. Neurosci.* 32, 7528–7537. 10.1523/JNEUROSCI.6352-11.2012

7. Croxson P. L., Walton M. E., O'Reilly J. X., Behrens T. E., Rushworth M. F. (2009). Effort-based cost-benefit valuation and the human brain. *J. Neurosci.* 29, 4531–4541. 10.1523/JNEUROSCI.4515-08.2009

8. Prevost C., Pessiglione M., Metereau E., Clery-Melin M. L., Dreher J. C. (2010). Separate valuation subsystems for delay and effort decision costs. *J. Neurosci.* 30, 14080–14090. 10.1523/JNEUROSCI.2752-10.2010

9. Lombardo, M. M., Eichinger, R. W. (1996). *The Career Architect Development Planner* (1st ed.). Minneapolis: Lominger.

10. https://www.702010forum.com/about-702010-framework Accessed 27th May 2015.

11. Sapra, S., Beavin, L. E., Zak, P. J. (2012). A combination of dopamine genes predicts success by professional Wall Street traders. *PLoS ONE*, 7, 1, e30844.

12. Perla, K., Alvarez-Lopez, M. J., Cosin-Tomas, M., Rosenkranz, M. A., Lutz, A., Davidson, R. J. 2014). Rapid changes in histone deacetylases and inflammatory gene expression in expert meditators. *Psychoneuroendocrinology*, 40, 96

13. Haas, B. W., Ishak, A., Anderson, I. W., Filkowski, M. M (2015). The tendency to trust is reflected in human brain structure. *Neurolmage*, 107, 175–181

14. Zak, P. J., Stanton, A. A., Ahmadi, S. (2007). Oxytocin increases generosity in humans. *Public Library of Science ONE*, 2, 11, e1128. doi:10.1371/journal.pone.0001128.

15. Cuddy, A. J. C., Wilmuth, C. A., Carney, D. R. (2012). "The Benefit of Power Posing Before a High-Stakes Social Evaluation." Harvard Business School Working Paper, No. 13-027

16. Zak, P. J., Kurzban, R., Ahmadi, S., Swerdloff, R. S., Park, J., Efremidze, L., Redwine, K., Morgan, K., Matzner, W. (2009). Testosterone administration decreases generosity in the ultimatum game. *PLoS ONE*, 4, 12. doi:10.1371/journal.pone.0008330.

17. Carney, D. R., Cuddy, A. J. C., Yap, A. J. (2010). Power posing: Brief nonverbal displays affect neuroendocrine levels and risk tolerance. *Psychological Science OnlineFirst*, September 21, doi: 10.1177

18. Weber, M., Webb, C. A., Deldonno, S. R., Kipman, M., Schwab, Z. J., Weiner, M. R. and Killgore, W. D. S. (2013), Habitual 'sleep credit' is associated with greater grey matter volume of the medial prefrontal cortex, higher emotional intelligence and better mental health. Journal of Sleep Research, 22: 527–534. doi: 10.1111/jsr.12056

19. Wagner, U. Gais, S., Haider, H., Verleger, R., Born, J. (2004). Sleep inspires insight. *Nature*. 427, 6792, 352–355

20. Maquet, P. (2001). The role of sleep in learning and memory. *Science*, 294, 1048–1052

21. Buzsáki, G. (1998). Memory consolidation during sleep: A neurophysiological perspective. *J. Sleep Res.* 7, Suppl. 1, 17–23
22. Xie et al. (2013). Sleep initiated fluid flux drives metabolite clearance from the adult brain. *Science*, October 18. DOI: 10.1126/science.1241224
23. Welsh, D. T., Ellis, A. P.J., Christian, M. S., Mai, K. M. (2014). Building a self-regulatory model of sleep deprivation and deception: The role of caffeine and social influence. *Journal of Applied Psychology.* 10; 00(6), 1268–1277
24. Drake, C., Roehrs, T., Shambroom, J., Roth T. (2013). Caffeine effects on sleep taken 0, 3, or 6 hours before going to bed. *J Clin Sleep Med*; 9, 11, 1195–1200.

2 Introducing the Winning Scientific Formula

1. D'Analeze, G., Dodge, T., Rayton, B. (2012) *The Evidence: Employee Engagement Taskforce, "Nailing the evidence" Workgroup.* Report. Engage For Success
2. Achor, S. (2011) *The Happiness Advantage: The Seven Principles of Positive Psychology that Fuel Success and Performance at Work.* London: Virgin Books
3. Daw, N. D., Shohamy, D. (2008) The cognitive neuroscience of motivation and learning. *Social Cognition,* 26:5: 593–620
4. Yin, H. H., Ostlund, S. B., Knowlton, B. J., Balleine, B. W. (2005) The role of the dorsomedial striatum in instrumental conditioning. *Eur. J. Neurosci.,* 22: 513–523.
5. Killcross, S., Coutureau, E. (2003) Coordination of actions and habits in the medial prefrontal cortex of rats. *Cereb. cortex,* 13: 400–408.
6. Damani, A., Tekchandaney, M. (2013) The surprising psychology of waiting in queues. March 11. *Behavioral Design.* Blog. https://behaviouraldesign.word-press.com/tag/behavioural-economics/ [Accessed March 6, 2015].

3 How Change Really Happens

1. Pascual-Leone, A., Amedi, A., Fregni, F., Merabet, L. B. (2005) The plastic human brain cortex. *Ann. Rev. Neurosci.,* 28: 377–401.
2. Pascual-Leone, A., Freitas, C., Oberman, L., Horvath, J. C., Halko, M., Eldaief, M. et al. (2011) Characterizing brain cortical plasticity and network dynamics across the age-span in health and disease with TMS-EEG and TMS-fMRI. *Brain Topogr.,* 24: 302–315.

3. Scholz, J., Klein, M. C., Behrens, T. E. (2009) Training induces changes in white-matter architecture. *Nat. Neurosci.,* 12:11, November: 1370–1371.
4. Maguire, E. A. et al. (2000) Navigation-related structural change in the hippocampi of taxi drivers. *PNAS,* 97: 4398–4403.
5. Draganski, B. Gaser, C., Busch, V., Schulerer, G., Bogdahn, U., May, A. (2004) Neuroplasticity: Changes in grey matter induced by training. *Nature,* 427: 311–312.
6. Driemeyer, J., Boyke, J., Gaser, C., Buchel, C., May, A. (2008) Changes in gray matter induced by learning-revisited. *PLoS One,* 3: e2669.
7. Posner, M. I., Tang, Y.-Y., Lynch, G. (2014) Mechanisms of white matter change induced by meditation training. *Front. Psychol.,* 5: 1220. doi:10.3389/fpsyg.2014.01220
8. Tang, Y., Posner, M. I. (2009) Attention training and attention state training. *Trends Cogn. Sci.,* 13: 222–227. doi:10.1016/j.tics.2009.01.009
9. Tang, Y. Y., Lu, Q., Fan, M., Yang, Y., Posner, M. I. (2012a) Mechanisms of white matter changes induced by meditation. *Proc. Natl. Acad. Sci. USA,* 109: 10570–10574. doi:10.1073/pnas.1207817109
10. Tang, Y. Y., Ma, Y., Wang, J., Fan, Y., Feng, S., Lu, Q., Sui, D., Rothbart, M. K., Fan, M., Posner, M. I. (2007) Short term meditation training improves attention and self regulation. *Proc. Natl. Acad. Sci. USA,* 104: 17152–17156. doi:10.1073/pnas.0707678104
11. Tang, Y. Y., Ma, Y., Fan, Y., Feng, H., Wang, J., Feng, S., et al. (2009) Central and autonomic nervous system interaction is altered by short term meditation. *Proc. Natl. Acad. Sci. USA,* 106: 8865–8870. doi:10.1073/pnas.0904031106
12. Bavelier, D., Levi, D. M., Li, R. W., Hench, T. K. (2010) Removing brakes on adult brain plasticity: from molecular to behavioural interventions. *J. Neurosci.,* 30:45: 14964–14971.
13. Bennett, E. L., Diamond, M. C., Krech, D., Rosenzweig, M. R. (1964) Chemical and anatomical plasticity of brain: Changes in brain through experience, demanded by learning theories, are found in experiments with rats. *Science,* 146:3644: 610–619.
14. Sale, A., Maya Vetencourt, J. F., Medini, P., Cenni, M. C., Baroncelli, L., De Pasquale, R., Maffie, L. (2007) Environmental enrichment in adulthood promotes amblyopia recovery through a reduction of intracortical inhibition. *Nat. Neurosci.,* 10: 679–681.
15. Bao, S., Chan, V. T., Merzenich, M. M. (2001) Cortical remodelling induced by activity of ventral tegmental dopamine neurons. *Nature,* 412:6842: 79–83.
16. Trei, L. (2007) New study yields instructive results on how mindset affects learning. Stanford Report, February 7. Website. http://news.stanford.edu/news/2007/february7/dweck-020707.html [Accessed March 10, 2015].

17. Eichenbaum, H. (2001) The hippocampus and declarative memory: Cognitive mechanisms and neural codes. *Behav. Brain Res.,* 127: 199–207.

18. Davachi, L., Wagner, A. D. (2002) Hippocampal contributions to episodic encoding: Insights from relational and item-based learning. *J. Neurophysiol.,* 88: 982–990.

19. Davachi, L., Mitchell, J. P., Wagner, A. D. (2003) Multiple routes to memory: Distinct medial temporal lobe processes build item and source memories. *Proc. Natl. Acad. Sci. USA.* 2157-2162, doi: 10.1073/pnas.0337195100

20. Lepage, M., Habib, R., Tulving, E. (1998) Hippocampal PET activations of memory encoding and retrieval: The HIPER model. *Hippocampus,* 8: 313–322.

21. Davachi, L., Dobbins, I. G. (2008) Declarative memory. *Association for Psychological Science,* 17:2: 112–118.

22. Eisenberger, N. L., Lieberman, M. D., Williams, K. D. (2003) Does rejection hurt? An fMRI study of social exclusion. *Science,* 302: 290–292.

23. Izuma, K., Saito, D. N., Sadato, N. (2008) Processing of social and monetary rewards in the human striatum. *Neuron,* 58: 294–294.

24. Posner, M. I., Petersen, S. E. (1990) The attention system of the human brain. *Ann. Rev. Neurosci.,* 13: 25–42.

25. Lavie, N. (2010) Attention, distraction and cognitive control under load. *Curr. Dir. Psychol.,* 19:3, June: 143–148.

26. Dye, M. W. G., Green, C. S., Bavelier, D. (2009) The development of attention skills in action video game players. *Neuropsychologia,* 47:8–9: 1780–1789.

27. Adcock, R. A. (2006) Reward-motivated learning: mesolimbic activation precedes memory formation. *Neuron,* 50: 507–517.

28. Harrison, Y., Horne, J. A. (1999) One night of sleep loss impairs innovative thinking and flexible decision making. *Organ Behav. Hum. Decis. Process* 78:2, May: 128–145.

29. Keen, C. (2006) Lack of sleep impairs job satisfaction, especially for women. UF News website. July 18. http://news.ufl.edu/archive/2006/07/uf-study-lack-of-sleep-impairs-job-satisfaction-especially-for-women.html [Accessed January 2015]

30. (2012) Can a lack of sleep make you behave unethically? Researchers think so. Virginia Tech Spotlight on Impact website. September 16. http://www.vt.edu/spotlight/impact/2012-09-17-sleep/barnes.html [Accessed January 2015]

31. Ding, Q., Ying, Z., Gomez-Pinilla, F. (2011) Exercise influences hippocampal plasticity by modulating brain-derived neurotrophic factor processing. *Neuroscience,* 192, 29 September: 773–780.

32. Agular, A. S. Jr., Castro, A. A., Moreira, E. L., Glaser, V., Santos, A. R., Tasca, C. L., Latini, A., Prediger, R. D. (2011) Short bouts of mild-intensity physical exercise improve spatial learning and memory in aging rats: Involvement of

hippocampal plasticity via AKT, CREB, and BDNF signaling. *Mech. Ageing Dev.*, 132:11–12, November–December: 560–567.

33. Colcombe, S. J., Kramer, A. F. (2003) Fitness effects on the cognitive function of older adults: a meta-analytic study. *Psychol. Sci.*, 14:2: 125–130.

34. Colcombe, S. J., Kramer, A. F., Erickson, K. I., Scalf, P., McAuley, E., Cohen, N. J. (2004) Cardiovascular fitness, cortical plasticity, and aging. *Proc. Natl. Acad. Sci. USA*, 101:9: 3316–3321.

35. Lombardo, M. M., Eichinger, R. W. (1996) *The Career Architect Development Planner* (1st ed.). Minneapolis: Lominger, p. iv.

36. Van der Heijden, K. B., Smits, M. G., Boudewijn Gunning, W. (2006) Sleep hygiene and actigraphically evaluated sleep characteristics in children with ADHD and chronic sleep onset insomnia. *J. Sleep Res.*, 15: 55–62.

37. Thorpy, M. (n.d.) Sleep hygiene. National Sleep Foundation website. http://sleepfoundation.org/ask-the-expert/sleep-hygiene [Accessed September 9, 2014].

Part II   How Do We Engage People?

1. CiPD (2008) *Employee Engagement: A CiPD Factsheet* (2007). London: The Chartered Institute of Personnel Development.

2. Conference Board (2006) *Employee Engagement: A Review of Current Research and its Implications*. New York: The Conference Board.

3. Arnsten, A. F. T. (1998) The biology of being frazzled. *Science*, 280: 1711–1712.

4. Friendman, R. S. Forster, J. (2001) The effects of promotion and prevention cues on creativity. *J. Pers. Soc. Psychol.*, 81:6: 1001–1013.

5. Jung-Beeman, M., Bowden, E.M., Haberman, J., Frymiare, J.L., Armbel-Liu, S., Greenblatt, R., Reber, P.J., Kounios, J. (2004) Neural activity when people solve verbal problems with insight. *PLoS Biology*, 2:4: 500–510.

6. Fredrickson, B. L. (2001) The role of positive emotions in positive psychology: The broaden-and-build theory of positive emotions. *Am. Psychol.*, 56: 218–226.

7. Schmitz, I. W., DeRosa, E., Anderson, A. K., (2009) Opposing influences of affective state valence on visual cortical encoding. *J. Neurosci.*, 29:22: 7199–7207.

4   The Concept You Have to Build Everything Else Around

1. Collins, J., Porras, J. (2005) *Built to Last: Successful Habits of Visionary Companies*. London: Random House Business

2. Malloch, T. R. (2011) *Doing Virtuous Business: The Remarkable Success of Spiritual Enterprise*. Nashville: Thomas Nelson

3. Sinek, S. (2011) *Start with Why: How Great Leaders Inspire Everyone to Take Action*. London: Penguin

4. Lyubomirsky, S., Sheldon, K. M., Schkade, D., 2005. Pursuing happiness: the architecture of sustainable change. Review of General Psychology 9, 111–131.

5. Moll, J., Krueger, F., Zahn, R., Pardini, M., Oliveria-Souza, R., Grafman, J. (2006) Human fronto-mesolimbic networks guide decisions about charitable donation. *Proc. Natl. Acad. Sci USA,* 103:42, 17 October: 15623–15628.

6. Deci, E. L. Ryan, R. M. (2000) The 'what' and 'why' of goal pursuit: Human needs and the self-determination of behavior. *Psychol. Inq.,* 11: 227–268.

7. Zak, P. J. and Barraza, J. A. (2013) Neurobiology of collective action. *Front. Neurosci.,* 7:211.

8. Aknin, L. B., Dunn, E. W., Whillans, A. V., Grant, A. M., Norton, M. I. (2013) Making a difference matters: Impact unlocks the emotional benefits of prosocial spending. *J. Econ. Behav. Organ.,* 88: 90–95.

9. Zahn, R. (2009) The neural basis of human social values: Evidence from functional MRI. *Cereb. Cortex,* 19:2, February 2009: 276–283.

10. Meier, S. Stutzer, A., (2008) Is volunteering rewarding in itself? *Economica,* 75: 39–59.

11. Lin, P.-Y., Grewal, N. S., Morin, C., Johnson, W. D., Zak, P. J. (2013) Oxytocin increases the influence of public service advertisements. *PLoS ONE,* 8: 2. doi: 10.1371/journal.pone.0056934.

12. Barraza, J. A., Alexander, V., Beavin, L. E., Terris, E. T., and Zak, P. J. (2015) The heart of the story: Peripheral physiology during narrative exposure predicts charitable giving. *Biol. Psychol.* 105:138–143

13. EY (2015) Our networks. EY website. http://www.ey.com/UK/en/About-us/Our-people-and-culture/Diversity-and-inclusiveness/About-EY---Diversity-and-inclusiveness---Our-networks [Accessed March 11, 2015]

14. Gerrig, R. J. (1993) *Experiencing Narrative Worlds: On the Psychological Activities of Reading*. New Haven: Yale University Press.

15. Crawford, D. (2013) Employee engagement in the 3rd sector – a time bomb waiting to explode? Cerus Consulting Report on People in Aid website. http://www.peopleinaid.org/pool/files/pubs/Employee-Engagement-in-the-3rd-Sector.pdf [Accessed March 9, 2015]

16. LaBar, K. S. Cabeza, R. (2006) Cognitive neuroscience of emotional memory. *Nat. Rev. Neurosci.,* 7: 54–64.

17. Damasio, A. (2006) *Descartes' Error*. London: Vintage Books

18. Tversky, A. Kahneman, D. (1973) Availability: A heuristic for judging frequency and probability. *Cogn. Psychol.,* 2: 207–32.

19. Murray, P. N. (2013) How emotions influence what we buy: The emotional core of consumer decision-making. *Inside the Consumer Mind* blog (February

26). Psychology Today website. https://www.psychologytoday.com/blog/inside-the-consumer-mind/201302/how-emotions-influence-what-we-buy [Accessed February 7, 2015].
20. Loftus, E. (2003) Our changeable memories: Legal and practical implications. *Nat. Rev. Neurosci.*, 4: 231–234.
21. Weinstein, N. Ryan, R. M. (2010) When helping helps: Autonomous motivation for prosocial behaviour and its influence on well-being for the helper and recipient. *J. Pers. Soc. Psychol.*, 98: 222–244.

5   The Jarring Awakening

1. Csikszentmihalyi, M. (1990) *Flow.* New York: HarperPerennial.
2. Kotler, S. (2014) *The Rise of Superman: Decoding the Science of Ultimate Human Performance.* Brilliance Corporation.
3. Nakamura, J., Csikszentmihalyi, M. (2001) Flow theory and research. In C. R. Snyder, E. Wright, S. J. Lopez (Eds.), *Handbook of Positive Psychology.* Oxford: Oxford University Press. pp. 195–206
4. Dietrich, A. (2004) Neurocognitive mechanisms underlying the experience of flow. *Consciousness and Cognition,* 13: 746–761
5. Eagleman, D. *Incognito: The Secret Lives of the Brain* (2012) Edinburgh: Canongate Books
6. Sherlin, L., Arns, M., Lubar, J., Heinrich, H., Kerson, C., Strehl, U., & Sterman, M. B. (2011). Neurofeedback and basic learning theory: Implications for research and practice. *J. Neurother. Invest. Neuromodul. Neurofeed. Appl. Neurosci., 15*:4: 292–304.
7. Goldberg, I., Harel, M., Malach, R. (2006) When the brain loses its self: Prefrontal inactivation during sensory-motor processing. *Neuron,* April 20,50:2: 329–339.
8. Limb, C. J. Braun, A. R. (2008) Neural substrates of spontaneous musical performance: An fMRI study of jazz improvisation. *PLoS ONE,* 3:2: e1679. doi:10.1371/journal.pone.0001679
9. Hawkins, J., Blakeslee, S. (2010) *On Intelligence.* New York: Times Books.
10. Zgierska, A., Rabago, D., Chawla, N., Kushner, K., Koehler, R., Marlatt, A. (2009) Mindfulness meditation for substance use disorders: A systematic review. *Subst. Abus.* (Systematic review), 30:4: 266–294.
11. Dane, E. Brummel, B. J. (2013) Examining workplace mindfulness and its relations to job performance and turnover intention. *Hum. Relat.,* 67:1: 105–128.
12. Brown, K. W. Ryan, R. M. (2003) The benefits of being present: Mindfulness and its role in psychological well-being. *J. Pers. Soc. Psychol.,* 84: 822–848

13. Rock, D. (2009) *Your Brain at Work*. New York: Harper Business.
14. Farb, N. A. S., Segal, Z. V., Mayber, H., Bean, J., McKeon, D., Fatima, Z., Anderson, A. K. (2007) Attending to the present: Mindfulness meditation reveals distinct neural modes of self-reference. *Soc. Cogn. Affect. Neurosci.* 2:4: 313–322.
15. Buckner, R. L., Andrews-Hanna, J. R., Schacter, D. L. (2008) The brain's default network: Anatomy, function, and relevance to disease. *Ann. NY Acad. Sci.*, 1124:1: 1–38.
16. Zeldan, F. Martucci, K. T., Kraft, R. A., Gordon, N. S., McHaffie, J. G., Coghill, R. C. (2011) Brain mechanisms supporting the modulation of pain by mindfulness meditation. *J. Neurosci.*, 31:14: 5540–5548.
17. Mental Health Foundation. (n.d.) Mental health statistics. Website. http://www.mentalhealth.org.uk/help-information/mental-health-statistics/ [Accessed February 3, 2015]
18. Khoury, B., Lecomte, T., Fortin, G., Masse, M., Therien, P., Bouchard, V., Hofmann, S. G. (2013) Mindfulness-based therapy: A comprehensive meta-analysis. *Clin. Psychol. Rev*, 33:6: 763–771.
19. Piet, J., Hougaard, E. (2011) The effect of mindfulness-based cognitive therapy for prevention of relapse in recurrent major depressive disorder: A systematic review and meta-analysis. *Clin. Psychol. Rev.*, 31:6: 1032–1040.
20. Paul, N. A., Stanton, S. J., Greeson, J. M., Smoski, M. J., Wang, L. (2013) Psychological and neural mechanisms of trait mindfulness in reducing depression vulnerability. *Soc. Cogn. Affect. Neurosci.* 8:1: 56–64.
21. Building the Case for Wellness (2008) PWC https://www.gov.uk/government/uploads/system/uploads/attachment_data/file/209547/hwwb-dwp-wellness-report-public.pdf [Accessed May 15, 2015]
22. Zeidan, F., et al. (2014) Neural correlates of mindfulness meditation-related anxiety relief *Soc. Cogn. Affect. Neurosci.*, 9:6: 751–759.
23. Haase, L., Thom, J. J., Shukia, A., Davenport, P. W., Simmons, A. N., Stanley, E. A., Paulus, M. P., Johnson, D. C. (2014) Mindulness-based training attenuates insula response to an aversive interoceptive challenge. *Soc. Cogn. Affect. Neurosci.*, 0:2014: nsu042v1–nsu042.
24. Goldin, P., Ziv, M., Jazaieri, H., Hahn, K., Gross, J. J. (2013) MBSR vs aerobic exercise in social anxiety: fMRI of emotion regulation of negative self-beliefs. *Soc. Cogn. Affect. Neurosci.* 8:1: 65–72.
25. Dorjee, D. (2013) *Mind, Brain and the Path to Happiness: A Guide to Buddhist Mind Training and the Neuroscience of Meditation*. London and New York: Routledge, p. 106
26. Lacaille, J., ally, J., Zacchia, N., Bourkas, S., Glaser, E., Knauper, B. (2014) The effects of three mindfulness skills on chocolate cravings. *Appetite*, 76: 101–112.

27. Taylor, V. A., Daneault, V., Grant, J., Scavone, G., Breton, E., Roffe-Vidal, S., Courtemanche, J., Lavarenne, A. S., Marrelec, G., Benali, H., Beauregard, M. (2013) Impact of meditation training on the default mode network during a restful state. *Soc. Cogn. Affect. Neurosci.* 8:1: 4–14

28. Kang, D., Jo, H. J., Jung, W. H., Kim, S. H., Jung, Y., Choi, C., Lee, U. S., An, S. C., Jang, J. H., Kwon, J. S. (2013) The effect of meditation on brain structure: Cortical thickness mapping and diffusion tensor imaging. *Soc. Cogn. Affect. Neurosci.* 8:1: 27–33.

29. Mascaro, J. S., Riling, J. K., Negi, L. T., Raison, C. L. (2013) Compassion meditation enhances empathic accuracy and related neural activity. *Soc. Cogn. Affect. Neurosci.* 8:1: 48–55.

30. Leung, M., Chan, C. C. H., Yin, J., Lee, C., So, K., Lee, T. M. C. (2013) Increased gray matter volume in the right angular and posterior parahippocampal gyri in loving-kindness meditators. *Soc. Cogn. Affect. Neurosci.* 8:1: 34–39.

31. Shapiro, S. L., Oman, D., Thoresen, C. E., Plante, T. G., Flinders, T. (2008), Cultivating mindfulness: Effects on well-being. *J. Clin. Psychol.*, 64:7: 840–862.

32. Davidson, R. J., Kabat-Zinn, J., Schumacher, J., Rosenkranz, M., Muller, D., Santorelli, S. F., Urbanowski, F., Harrington, A., Bonus, K., Sheridan, J. F. (2003), Alterations in brain and immune function produced by mindfulness meditation. *Psychosom. Med.*, 65: 567–570.

33. Karelaia, N. (2014) How mindfulness improves decision-making. *INSEAD Knowledge* blogpost, August 5, Forbes website. http://www.forbes.com/sites/insead/2014/08/05/how-mindfulness-improves-decision-making/ [Accessed March 23, 2015].

6   The Reassuring Truth

1. Baumeister, R. F., Leary, M. R. (1995) The need to belong: Desire for interpersonal attachments as a fundamental human motivation. *Psychol. Bull.*, 117: 497–529.

2. Eisenberger, N. I., Lieberman, M. D. (2004) Why rejection hurts: A common neural alarm system for physical and social pain. *Trends Cogn. Sci.*, 8: 294–300.

3. Cacioppo, J. T., Patrick, W. (2008) *Loneliness: Human Nature and the Need for Social Connection*. New York: WW Norton.

4. Zak, P. J. (2005) Trust: A temporary human attachment facilitated by oxytocin. *Behav. Brain Sci.*, 28:3: 368–369.

5. Gonzales, A. L., Hancock, J. T., Pennebaker, J. W. (2010) Language style matching as a predictor of social dynamics in small groups. *Commun. Res.*, 37:1: 3–19.
6. Niederhoffer, K. G., Pennebaker, J. W. (2002) Linguistic style matching in social interaction. *J. Lang. Soc. Psychol.*, 21: 337–360. doi:10.1177/026192702237953
7. Niederhoffer, K. G., Pennebaker, J. W. (2009) Sharing one's story: On the benefits of writing or talking about emotional experience. In S. J. Lopez C. R. Snyder (Eds.), *Oxford Handbook of Positive Psychology* (2nd ed.). New York: Oxford University Press. pp. 621–632.
8. O'Donnell, M. B., Falk, E. B., Lieberman, M. D. (in press) Social in, social out: How the brain responds to social language with more social language. *Commun. Monogr.*
9. Meyer, M. L., Masten, C. L., Ma, Y., Wang, C., Shi, Z., Eisenberger, N. I., Lieberman, M. D., Han, S. (in press) Differential neural activation to friends and strangers links interdependence to empathy. *Culture and Brain.*
10. Morelli, S. A., Lieberman, M. D., and Zaki, J. (in press) The emerging study of positive empathy. *Social and Personality Psychology Compass.*
11. Wallace, B. A., Shapiro, S. L. (2006) Mental balance and well-being: Building bridges between Buddhism and western psychology. *Am. Psychol.*, 61:7: 690.
12. Fredrickson, B. L. (2001) The role of positive emotions in positive psychology: The broaden-and-build theory of positive emotions. *Am. Psychol.*, 56:3, 218.
13. Varnum, M. E., Shi, Z., Chen, A., Qiu, J., Han, S. (2014) When 'your' reward is the same as 'my' reward: Self-construal priming shifts neural responses to own vs. friends' rewards. *NeuroImage*, 87: 164–169.
14. Morelli, S. A., Lieberman, M. D. (2013) The role of automaticity and attention in neural processes underlying empathy for happiness, sadness, and anxiety. *Front. Hum. Neurosci.*, 7, doi: 10.3389/fnhum.2013.00160.
15. Tabak, B. A., Meyer, M. L., Castle, E., Dutcher, J. M., Irwin, M. R., Han, J. H., Lieberman, M. D., Eisenberger, N. I. (2015) Vasopressin, but not oxytocin, increases empathic concern among individuals who received higher levels of paternal warmth: A randomized controlled trial. *Psychoneuroendocrinology*, 51: 253–261.
16. Fischer-Shofty, M., Levkovitz, Y., Shamay-Tsoory, S. G. (2012) Oxytocin facilitates accurate perception of competition in men and kinship in women. *Soc. Cogn. Affect. Neurosci.*, 8:3: 313.
17. Falk, E. B., Morelli, S. A., Welborn, B. L., Dambacher, K., Lieberman, M. D. (2013) Creating buzz: The neural correlates of effective message propagation. *Psychol. Sci.*, 24; 1234–1242.

18. Stephens, G. J., Silbert, L. J., Hasson, U. (2010) Speaker-listener neural coupling underlies successful communication. *Proc. Natl. Acad. Sci. USA,* 107: 14425–14430.

Part III   How Do We Motivate People?

1. Laloux, F., (2014) *Reinventing Organizations,* Nelson Parker.

7   The Synaptic Circle

1. Haggard, P. (2008) Human volition: Towards a neuroscience of will. *Nat. Rev. Neurosci.,* 9: 934–946. Retrieved from The Brain and The Mind website. http://thebrainandthemind.co.uk/Build/Assets/readings/Human%20 Volition%20Patrick%20Haggard.pdf [Accessed March 20, 2015]
2. Libet, B. (1985) Unconscious cerebral initiative and the role of conscious will in voluntary action. *Behav. Brain Sci.,* 8: 529–566.
3. Donny, E. C., Bigelow, G. E., Walsh, S. L. (2006) Comparing the physiological and subjective effects of self-administered vs yoked cocaine in humans. *Psychopharmacology,* 186:4: 544–552.
4. Dworkin, S. I., Mirkis, S., Smith, J. E. (1995). Response-dependent versus response-independent presentation of cocaine: differences in the lethal effects of the drug. *Psychopharmacology,* 117:3: 262–266.
5. LeDoux, J. (2003) *The Synaptic Self: How Our Brains Become Who We Are.* London & New York: Penguin
6. Hawkins, J., Blakeslee, S. (2004) *On Intelligence: How a New Understanding of the Brain Will Lead to the Creation of Truly Intelligent Machines.* New York: Times Books.
7. Hedden, T., Gabrieli, J. D. E. (2006). The ebb and flow of attention in the human brain. *Nat. Neurosci.,* 9: 863–865.

8   Are You Capitalizing on a Neuro-friendly Culture?

1. Greenleaf, R. K. [1977] (2002). *Servant Leadership: A Journey into the Nature of Legitimate Power and Greatness* (25th anniversary ed.). New York: Paulist Press, 24.

2. Zak, P. (2013) *The Moral Molecule: The New Science of What Makes Us Good or Evil*. London: Corgi
3. Card, D., Mas, A., Moretti, E., Saez, E. (2012) Inequality at work: The effect of peer salaries on job satisfaction. *American Economic Review* 102: 2981–3003.
4. Tabibnia, G., Lieberman, M.D. (2007) Fairness and cooperation are rewarding: Evidence from social cognitive neuroscience. *New York Academy of Sciences*, 1118: 90–101.
5. Daw, N. D., Shohamy, D., (2008) The cognitive neuroscience of motivation and learning. *Soc. Cognition*, 26:5: 593–620

9 Your Fundamental Checklist for Behavioral Success

1. Kahneman, D. (2011) *Thinking, Fast and Slow*. London & New York: Penguin.
2. Drevets, W. C., Raichle, M. E. (1998) Suppression of regional cerebral blood flow during emotional versus higher cognitive processes: Implications for interactions between emotion and cognition. *Cogn. Emotion*, 12: 353–385.
3. McClure, S. M., Laibson, D. I., Loewenstein, G., Cohen, J. D. (2004) Separate neural systems value immediate and delayed monetary rewards. *Science*, 306:5695: 503–507
4. Goel, V., Dolan, R. J. (2003) Explaining modulation of reasoning by belief. *Cognition*, B11–B22
5. Dolcos, F., McCarthy, G. (2006) Brain systems mediating cognitive interference by emotional distraction. *J. Neurosci.*, 26:7: 2072–2079.
6. Drew, T., Vo, M. L.-H., Wolfe, J. M. (2013) The invisible gorilla strikes again: Sustained inattential blindness in expert observers. *Psychol. Sci.*
7. Eastwood, J. D., Frischen, A., Fenske, M. J., Smilek, D. (2012) The unengaged mind: Defining boredom in terms of attention. *Perspect. Psychol. Sci.*, 7: 482–95.
8. Hausman, D. M., Welch. B. (2010) Debate: To nudge or not to nudge. *J. Polit. Philos.*, 18:1: 123–136.
9. Thaler, R. H., Sunstein, C. R. (2008) *Nudge: Improving Decisions About Health, Wealth and Happiness*. New Haven & London: Yale University Press.
10. Dolan, P., et al. (2012) Influencing behaviour the MINDSPACE way. *J. Econ. Pychol.*, 33: 264–277.
11. Kahneman, D., Tversky, A. (1979) Prospect theory: An analysis of decisions under risk. *Econometrica*, 47:2: 263–291.
12. Furnham, A., Boo, H. C. (2011) A literature review of the anchoring effect. *The Journal of Socio-Economics*, 40: 35–42.

13. Schenkel, B., Schuldt-Jensen, J., Rathmann Jensen, A., Guldborg Hansen, P. (2015) Even Danish CEOs can fall prey to judgment error. *i Nudge you* blogpost, January 22. http://inudgeyou.com/anchoring/ [Accessed March 16, 2015]
14. Rasul, I., Hollywood, D. (2012) Can nudges help to cut household energy consumption? *Guardian sustainable business* blogpost, January 27. *The Guardian* website. http://www.theguardian.com/sustainable-business/behaviour-change-energy-consumption [Accessed March 16, 2015]
15. Rithalia, A., McDaid, C., Suekarran, S., Myers, L., Sowden, A. (2009) Impact of presumed consent for organ donation on donation rates: a systematic review. *Brit. Med. J.*, 338.
16. Birnback, D., King, D., Vlaev, I., Rosen, L.F., Harvey, P.D. (2013) Impact of environmental olfactory cues on hand hygiene behaviour in a simulated hospital environment: A randomized study. *Journal of Hospital Infection.*
17. Gine, X., Karland, D., Sinman, J. (2010) Put your money where your butt is: A commitment contract for smoking cessation. *American Economic Journal: Applied Economics*, 2: 213–235.
18. Holland, Hendriks, Aarts (2005) Smells like clean spirit: Nonconscious effects of scent on cognition and behavior. *Psychol. Sci.*, 16: 689–693.
19. Dijksterhuis, Bargh (2001) The perception-behaviour expressway: Automatic effects of social perception on social behaviour. *Adv. Exp. Soc. Psychol.*, 33: 1–40.
20. Wryobeck, Chen, (2003) Using priming techniques to facilitate health behaviours. *Clinical Psychologist*, 7: 105–108.
21. Winkleman, Berridge, Wilbarger (2005) Unconscious affective reactions to masked happy versus angry faces influence consumption behavior and judgments of value. *Pers. Soc. Psychol. B.*, 31:1: 121–135.
22. Sharot, T. (2011) *The Optimism Bias: A Tour of the Irrationally Positive Brain.* New York: Pantheon
23. Sharot, T. (2012) The Optimism Bias by Tali Sharot: extract. January 1. *The Guardian* website. http://www.theguardian.com/science/2012/jan/01/tali-sharot-the-optimism-bias-extract [Accessed March 17, 2015]
24. Koo, M., Fishbach, A. (2012) The small-area hypothesis: Effects of progress monitoring on goal adherence. *J. Consum. Res.*, 39: 493–509

10 Managing for...

1. Kringelbach, M. L., Berridge, K. C. (2009) Towards a functional neuroanatomy of pleasure and happiness. *Trends Cogn. Sci.*, 13:11: 479–487

2. Oswald, A. J., Proto, E., Sgroi, D.(2009) *Happiness and Productivity.* IZA Discussion Paper No. 4645, December. Bonn: Institute for the Study of Labor

3. Deaton, A. (2011) The financial crisis and the well-being of Americans: 2011. OEP Hicks Lecture. *Oxford Econ. Pap.,* 64: 1–26

4. Schwarz, N., Strack, F., Mai, H.-P. (1991) Assimilation and contrast effects in part-whole question sequences: A conversational logic analysis. *Public Opin. Quart.,* 55: 3–23

5. Seligman, M. E., Steen, T. A., Park, N., Peterson, C. (2005) Positive psychology progress: Empirical validation of interventions. *Am. Psychol.,* 60:5: 410–421

6. Kringelbach, M. L., Berridge, K. C. (2010) The neuroscience of happiness and pleasure. *Soc. Res.,* 77: 2: 659–678.

7. Kringelbach, M. L. (2004) Emotion. In R. L. Gregory (Ed.), *The Oxford Companion to the Mind.* 2. Oxford: Oxford University Press. pp. 287–290

8. Ashby, F. G., Isen, A. M., Turken, A. U. (1999) A neuropsychological theory of positive affect and its influence on cognition. *Psychol. Rev.,* 106:3: 529–550.

9. Sacks, O. (2006) The power of music. *Brain,* 129: 2528–2532.

10. Koelsch, S. (2010) Towards a neural basis of music-evoked emotions. *Trends Cogn. Sci.,* 14: 131–137.

11. Weir, K. (2011) The exercise effect. *Monitor on Psychology,* 42: 11. Retrieved from American Psychological Association website. http://www.apa.org/monitor/2011/12/exercise.aspx [Accessed March 9, 2015]

12. Fowler, J. H., Christakis, N. A. (2008) The dynamic spread of happiness in a large social network. *Brit. Med. J.,* 337: a2338.

13. Dweck, C. (2007) *Mindset: The New Psychology of Success.* New York: Ballantine Books

14. Benson, H., Proctor, W. (2004) *The Breakout Principle: How to Activate the Natural Trigger that Maximizes Creativity, Athletic Performance, Productivity, and Personal Well-being.* New York: Scribner

15. Dane, E., Pratt, M. G. (2007) Exploring intuition and its role in managerial decision making. *Acad. Manage. Rev.,* 32: 33–54.

16. Karelaia, N., Reb, J. (Forthcoming) Improving decision making through mindfulness. In J. Reb, P. W. B. Atkins (Eds.) *Mindfulness in Organizations: Foundations, Research, and Applications.* Cambridge: Cambridge University Press.

17. Parkinson, B., Simons, G. (2009) Affecting others: Social appraisal and emotion contagion in everyday decision making. *Pers. Soc. Psychol. B.,* 35: 1071–1084

18. Jung, R. E., Mead, B. S., Carrasco, J., Flores, R. A. (2013) The structure of creative cognition in the human brain. *Front. Hum. Neurosci.* 7: 330.

19. Baird. B., et al. (2012) Inspired by distraction: Mind wandering facilitates creative incubation. *Psychol. Sci.,* 23: 1117–1122.
20. Dietrich, A., Audiffren, M. (2011) The reticular-activating hypofrontality (RAH) model of acute exercise. *Neurosci. Biobehav. Rev.,* 35: 1305–1325.
21. Robinson-Riegler, B., Robinson-Riegler, G. (2012) *Cognitive Psychology: Applying the Science of the Mind* (3rd ed.). Boston: Pearson Allyn & Bacon.
22. Kounios, J., Beeman, M. (2009) The aha! moment: The cognitive neuroscience of insight. *Curr. Dir. Psychol. Sci.,* 18: 4: 210–216.
23. Jung-Beeman, M., Bowden, E. M., Haberman, J., Frymiare, J. L., Arambel-Liu, S., Greenblatt, R., Reber, P. J., Kounios, J. (2004) Neural activity when people solve verbal problems with insight. *PLoS Biology,* 2: 4: 500–510.

Index